Intro-
duction
to
Program-
matic
Advertising

Dominik Kosorin

ISBN: 978-80-260-9611-5

For Zuzana and Samuel

CONTENTS

ACKNOWLEDGMENTS

My wife Zuzana, who supported me patiently and enthusiastically while working on this book. Matej Novak and Zuzana Neupauerova, whose infectious passion for programmatic advertising made this book possible, and the best it could be. Jana Tkacikova, who has an eye for making things better. Anezka Hruba Ciglerova, who designed a fresh and original book cover.

INTRODUCTION

Programmatic advertising is the most exciting thing that happened in marketing in a long time – perhaps since the advent of mass advertising itself. For the purpose of this book, programmatic advertising is defined as the automation of buying and selling of ad inventory, supported by the OpenRTB ecosystem. While this might sound like a mere evolutionary step, its implications are in fact revolutionary.

The automation of ad inventory trading process is a foundation, enabling a completely new approach to marketing communication. In a world where each impression can be individually bought and sold, data comes to the forefront to help make good trading decisions. In fact, automation technology is designed to derive its power from data. In the programmatic revolution, marketers who have access to high-quality data, and know how to use it, win.

For the first time in human history, mass advertising can be individually tailored, transforming it into true one-on-one communication. As a marriage of automation and data, programmatic advertising lets marketers take advantage of everything they know about the user who is about to view an ad, and customize the experience on the fly.

For example, a car manufacturer can communicate in a certain way with people who are in the market for a new car (and are perhaps considering a competitor's product), and offer a different message to someone who has been a loyal customer for ten years. With more data and increasingly sophisticated algorithms to make it actionable, reaching the right people at the right time with the right message has never been easier.

Having started as a disruptive technology at the low-end of display ad inventory, programmatic advertising is now quickly maturing. New formats are becoming available, which go beyond the standard banner ad – most notably rich media, video and native. Programmatic is being adapted for new channels as well, including TV, audio, out-of-home or print. With more premium ad inventory that can be bought across various channels, it is no longer an exclusive domain of performance advertisers. Today, very engaging branding campaigns can be executed through automated channels as well. Supported by the right data, campaign impact and efficiency can be potentially unparalleled.

Apart from the obvious cost savings and increased efficiency which can be achieved through automation and careful targeting, programmatic offers further benefits. With more ad inventory becoming available through automated channels, campaigns can be increasingly managed from a single central point. As a result, marketers (or increasingly algorithms on their behalf) can pick not just the right messages, but also their format, channel, order and frequency for each individual recipient. Such level of control across channels has never been possible before. Programmatic advertising is clearly a big deal, and is here to stay and evolve.

This book is intended as an introductory overview of the new and rapidly changing world of programmatic. It was written with people who are new to the technology in mind – some digital experience can be helpful, but is not strictly required. The aim is to offer an opportunity to quickly get up to speed with the basics of programmatic advertising, common terminology, and issues which resonate throughout the industry. As noted previously, the scope of this book is mainly OpenRTB ecosystem – closed programmatic advertising systems (offered for example by Facebook or Google) are not covered.

Book overview

Chapter one outlines the basic technologies enabling programmatic advertising, including cookies, pixels, banner ads, ad servers, networks and exchanges. Having a firm grasp of the basics is key to understanding more advanced concepts further in the book.

Chapter two opens the door into the world of programmatic proper, introducing various players in the ecosystem. On the buy side, we will explore advertisers, demand-side platforms, and agency trading desks. On the sell side, publishers (and publisher co-ops) will be explored, along with supply-side platforms. This chapter also introduces data management platforms, data/fraud/viewability vendors, as well as important industry bodies and other regulators.

Chapter three delves into the details of programmatic ad trading. We will look at auction-based as well as fixed price transaction types, and the enabling OpenRTB and OpenDirect protocols. Special attention is given to real-time bidding (RTB) auction, which has to some extent become synonymous with programmatic advertising. The deal ID and inventory monetization strategies (including header bidding) will be covered in chapter three as well.

Chapter four is dedicated to data (audience data in particular), a key ingredient giving programmatic advertising its power. General data classification based on source (first-, second- or third-party) and collection method (declared, inferred or modelled) will set the stage, followed by overview of the typical data application – ad targeting. Retargeting will be explored in depth, followed by prospecting tactics such as contextual targeting, behavioral targeting, and look-a-like modelling.

Chapter five is fairly short, but very important – expanding the programmatic advertising discussion into mobile. Mobile devices have their peculiarities, especially when it comes to cookies, in-app vs. mobile browser environments, or ad formats. Mobile offers new opportunities for programmatic though, coming from cross-device identification solutions or location data availability.

Chapter six gives an overview of current issues discussed across the industry. Fraud, viewability and attribution need to be solved to increase advertiser confidence and trust. From user perspective, ad blocking and privacy are very important concerns.

Chapter seven covers new formats and channels, which are becoming available programmatically at a breakneck pace. These include premium, highly engaging audiovisual formats such as rich media or video, as well as native ads. TV, audio, out-of-home and print form the next frontier of automation.

1 BASIC TECHNOLOGIES

In order to make sense of programmatic advertising, one must first have a firm grasp of some very basic technologies which lie at its core. This chapter will therefore give a quick overview of cookies & pixels, banner ads, ad servers, networks and exchanges. Of course, this is just a selection of the most critical foundational bits common to all display advertising (not just programmatic), rather than an exhaustive technology overview. More advanced concepts and technologies will be explored in later chapters of this book. Without first understanding the basics though, the following chapters could become slightly confusing.

Cookies

A cookie (also known as HTTP cookie or browser cookie) is a small piece of data sent from a web server and stored in a web browser. Every time a web browser makes a request to a server, this data is sent back to the server along with the request. As the request is fulfilled, web server can update cookie in the browser as well.

Cookie data is stored in a text file, and can be read only by the server domain which set it. Every web browser manages its own cookies. This means that a single internet user might have multiple cookies from the same domain (in Google Chrome as well as Mozilla Firefox for example). Cookies are independent, so in this case the same user appears as two distinct individuals to a web server.

The reason cookies were invented and are very useful today is maintaining state of a browser session - keeping track of all the user activity related to a particular browser and domain. The HTTP protocol is stateless by design, which means that without cookies, a web server would treat every request as an isolated event. Cookies let the web server know that some requests are related, and can provide additional information that is helpful when fulfilling them.

Cookies come in two basic flavors – session cookies and persistent cookies. Session cookies are used to store temporary state, and are usually deleted when the web browser is closed. They don't have a set expiration date, so the browser knows they are session cookies. Persistent cookies, on the other hand, are used to keep state over an extended period of time. They exist until a set expiration date is reached (which can be months or years), and are therefore very useful for user tracking.

When set, cookies usually have the same domain attribute as the domain that a user is currently visiting – these are called first-party cookies. However, if a web page contains content from other domains (typically banner ads), cookies with a different domain attribute can be set as well. These are called third-party cookies, and can be read by the domain that set them. Third-party cookies can be used to easily track users across multiple domains, and are controversial with regards to data control and privacy. They can be blocked in most browsers, rendering them unsuitable for common analytics applications. Web analytics vendors therefore use first-party cookies instead.

So what are some practical applications of cookies?

First of all, cookies are used to identify users. When a user visits a page for the first time, the web server saves a cookie in their browser. From this point on (until the cookie is deleted or expires), the server can identify all requests coming from the same user. If the user has logged in, their cookie is used to keep track of the logged-in state.

Cookies also enable storing user information and preferences. For example, a cookie might be used to keep track of an online shopping basket – contents, quantities, timestamps etc. This data can be stored in the cookie itself (client-side), and sent to the web server with each request. Typically, though, data is saved in a database on the server (server-side), and cookie is used for matching data to a particular user. This way, the server knows the state of the shopping basket for this user, and can display it properly with each page request.

An important use of cookies (particularly in the context of programmatic advertising) is user tracking. Cookies enable compilation of browsing history on a particular domain, or even across domains. This is invaluable for analytics – knowing exactly how users interact with a website, for instance, makes it possible to improve user experience over time. Tracking is also behind user segmentation – if, for example, the browsing history reveals that a particular user has visited car-related websites multiple times over the last week, they might fall into a "car interest" or even "car purchase intender" behavioral segments.

For cookies to be truly useful in the programmatic ecosystem, they need to be synchronized between the various players. Cookie synching is a bit more advanced concept at this point, so it will be covered later in chapter four.

Cookie issues

A common concern with regards to browser cookies is the lifespan. Cookies are often blocked or deleted on a regular basis, preventing them from keeping state over an extended period of time. Attempts have been made to overcome this problem with so-called "zombie cookies" – these use backups outside of the main cookie storage, and simply recreate any deleted cookies. Naturally, such practice is highly controversial, denying users the right to protect their privacy by deleting unwanted cookies.

Cookies are also becoming less and less useful when it comes to user identification. A typical user might be using multiple desktop browsers along with a smartphone (where cookie-free apps are prevalent) or other devices. It is hard to piece together such a fragmented browsing history, and cross-device identification that goes beyond cookies is consequently becoming a hot topic.

Last but not least, cookies are becoming synonymous with privacy violation among the general public. There was very little education about cookies and their benefits in the past, and users were mostly oblivious to their existence. Cookie misuse, particularly with regards to third-party cookies, has led to increased regulation and concern.

These and other issues contribute to what is sometimes referred to as "the crumbling cookie". It is clear that cookies will be at some point replaced by another technology. In the meantime, though, they are behind much of ad tech as we know it today.

Pixels

A tracking pixel (also known as tag, bug or beacon) is a piece of code embedded in an email or a web page, in order to track user activity. A tracking pixel is usually implemented as a tiny, invisible image (1x1, or one pixel), referenced through a single line of HTML code. Alternatively, JavaScript can be used for the same purpose. Tracking pixels are typically used for email marketing (to see if emails are opened, by whom and when), and for web analytics.

When a web page is loaded, a tracking pixel will fire with request to a web server. This request can contain a lot of useful information – such as time of the request, IP address, or whether any cookies from the web server have been previously set. This information is logged, and the server can set cookies.

Tracking pixels are often used by third parties in order to track user activity on a particular site. Beyond the typical implementations noted above, any external content on a website can serve as a tracking pixel – including banner ads or social media buttons. Requests fired by the pixels go to a third-party web server, enabling it to set third-party cookies. For publishers, it is therefore extremely important to know which tracking pixels are allowed on their web sites, to protect their valuable data and user privacy.

In order to manage tracking pixels on a web site efficiently, publishers often implement a tag management system (such as Google Tag Manager or Adobe's Dynamic Tag Management). Such systems offer a simple user interface, and require only initial implementation by the IT department. After that, tracking pixels can be easily added or removed by the responsible team (such as digital marketing).

Banner ads

Banner ad is a common form of display advertising, and an important building block of the programmatic ecosystem today. The bulk of advertising inventory available programmatically can be used to serve banner ads, which range from static (text or graphic) to video and rich media.

Standard banner ads typically appear along the top, the bottom, or sides of a webpage on desktop. On mobile, popular placements for banners are along the top of the page, or further down the page embedded within content. Most common desktop formats include 300x250 pixels (Medium Rectangle), 728x90 pixels (Leaderboard) and 160x600 pixels (Wide Skyscraper). On mobile, 320x50 pixels and 300x250 pixels are popular formats. The IAB (Interactive Advertising Bureau) provides detailed specifications and guidelines for the proper use of banner ads.

The banner ad creative is an important consideration in programmatic. In the past, banner ads for a campaign would typically comprise of one or just a handful of creatives, served to everyone without distinction. With the advent of dynamic advertising, content of a banner ad can be generated and personalized on the fly as the webpage loads – based on data about the user who is about to see the ad. A typical use case for dynamic creative is product retargeting, where users are shown recently viewed products within the banner ad. However, possibilities are much broader – including storytelling, or personalization for different audiences.

Common issues related to banner ads include fraud and viewability concerns (discussed in chapter six), inventory quality, as well as general dislike for this form of advertising – manifested in the rise of adblocking. Banner ads are getting to some extent replaced by native advertising on mobile, where browser usage is low and users prefer apps. For many advertisers, impact and ROI of display advertising remains unclear, due in part to the proliferation of last-click attribution models (attribution is discussed later in a separate section). On the bright side, banner ads are constantly developing and new, engaging formats are being introduced (grouped under the rich media umbrella, covered in chapter seven). It remains to be seen whether banner ads have their best years behind them – though they are certainly still going strong at the moment.

Ad servers

An ad server is a server, used for delivery of digital ads. Apart from serving ads, ad servers can fulfill a number of other roles, including campaign trafficking and management, optimization, metric tracking, reporting, and post-campaign analysis.

Two broad categories of ad servers exist – publisher ad servers and advertiser ad servers. For publishers, an ad server is used to manage and prioritize simultaneous campaigns from multiple clients. For advertisers, an ad server enables centralized campaign management across different media and publishers. Advertisers typically rely on third-party ad servers, operated by independent companies. DSPs are increasingly offering ad serving functionality as well.

Ad networks

An ad network is a company specializing in aggregating inventory from different publishers and selling it on to advertisers on their behalf. The ad network acts as a broker for advertising space, making it easier for publishers to participate in the market, and for advertisers to run large campaigns across many publishers. A typical ad network business model is to purchase inventory from publishers, package it, and sell it with a markup.

Transparency has been one of the biggest issues with ad networks. Advertisers often don't know where exactly will their ads appear, and what is the markup a network charges on the inventory. Also, picking and managing ad networks has become increasingly complicated, due to the sheer number of competitors in this space. Due to these and other issues, ad networks are now taking a back seat as programmatic trading supported by ad exchanges grows in popularity.

Ad exchanges

An ad exchange is a marketplace for advertising inventory, based on an automated auction technology. Ad exchanges enable real-time auction of each impression as it becomes available, selling it to the highest bidder. This is great for publishers, since their inventory is in theory sold for the maximum possible price. Ad exchanges also benefit advertisers, letting them decide how much each impression is worth to them (often based on additional data) and bid accordingly. This way, advertisers are in control of the scale and the efficiency of their campaigns in a more transparent fashion. Ad exchanges can be accessed via DSPs, or other bidding technologies.

2 PROGRAMMATIC ADVERTISING ECOSYSTEM

Programmatic advertising ecosystem can be broadly divided into two distinct parts – buy side and sell side.

On the buy side, we have advertisers who purchase ad inventory for their campaigns. To do so, they usually either set up their own in-house programmatic team, or employ an agency or agency trading desk to manage programmatic buying on their behalf. Programmatic inventory buying is supported by demand-side platforms (DSPs) or custom bidders, which can participate in an open real-time bidding auction.

On the sell side are the publishers or publisher co-ops, who provide ad inventory on their properties. Publishers offer their inventory programmatically either through supply-side platforms (SSPs), or via ad exchanges.

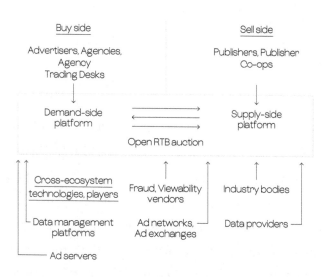

Programmatic advertising ecosystem

Some parts of the ecosystem span both buy- and sell-sides. A key advantage of programmatic advertising is the ability to use data to increase campaign efficiency and inform inventory trading decisions. Both the sell-side as well as buy-side players can collect and take advantage of user data, which is typically facilitated through a demand-side platform (DSP). There are other shared components of the programmatic ecosystem as well, including various data, fraud and viewability vendors. Industry bodies and governments also play a key role in regulation, standardization and development of the ecosystem.

Let us now look at some of the programmatic advertising ecosystem participants in more detail, starting with the buy side.

Advertisers

Advertisers are the ones fuelling the rapid growth of programmatic, and doing so with an increasing appetite. Their case for this trend is clear – higher advertising efficiency through automation and data. With unparalleled reach, access to premium inventory, engaging rich media formats and video, as well as solutions for fraud and viewability issues, programmatic is now very attractive for both performance and branding advertisers alike.

Performance advertisers were the early adopters of programmatic, since the ability to target individual users and optimize over time far outweighed initially lower inventory quality and other issues. For performance advertisers, the return on investment is key, as they tailor their campaigns towards measurable conversions. Branding advertisers are not as focused on direct impact though, but rather aim to build brand awareness and preference over time. Programmatic advertising has come a long way since the early days to become a very impactful, brand-safe environment. In addition to the open marketplace, cautious advertisers can take advantage of private marketplaces or programmatic direct.

For advertisers, the really exciting part of the current shift to programmatic is the data layer behind it. They can know their customers and prospects like never before, and tailor their advertising efforts on the individual level. This is a huge shift from the anonymous, affinity-based mass marketing communication of the past, with the potential that is still difficult to fully grasp. Programmatic makes efficient one-to-one marketing communication possible on an unprecedented scale, across many digital channels and formats.

Most advertisers have already moved beyond the discovery of retargeting (reaching out to users the advertiser already knows, typically because they already visited their website), and are exploring prospecting opportunities with their second- and third-party data partners. However, this is still just early days, and the best data approaches are currently being tested and developed. More sophisticated advertisers are working on long-term data ownership, integration, analysis and enablement strategies, encompassing data from their own properties, partners or advertising campaigns. In the long run, data will allow advertisers to gradually improve everything from impression-level media selection and tailored creatives all the way to their actual products and services. Data levels the playing field, giving smart advertisers – albeit with smaller media budgets – a fair chance to compete and win.

Executing a successful programmatic and data strategy requires attracting the right talent though, along with a suitable technology and partners. Many large advertisers have decided to move everything – from programmatic media buying to data management – in-house, and to develop a strategic competency in this area. Others work with their agencies and agency trading desks, or DSP managed services teams.

Attribution and accountability remain an issue for both performance and branding advertisers. Click-through rate (CTR) is still widely used as an efficiency metric, but mostly due to the convenience and a lack of understanding. Performance advertisers are increasingly moving towards real (and hard to manipulate) metrics such as conversions and return on investment (ROI). For brand advertisers though, metrics such as reach, frequency, or awareness/purchase intent uplift are more suitable. Moreover, they can be augmented with data and technology to account for viewability, fraud or on-target accuracy.

Demand side platforms

A demand side platform (or DSP) is a gateway to the programmatic world for agencies and advertisers. DSPs are used to purchase advertising in an automated way on a wide range of inventory – including ad exchanges, ad networks or SSPs. Demand side platforms serve as a central point of programmatic campaigns, enabling the design, execution, optimization and subsequent analysis of a media strategy.

DSPs are great in giving buyers a lot of control over their programmatic campaign strategies, often executed through a real-time bidding auction. Parameters such as budgets, maximum bids, timing, frequency, inventory or geography can be set according to campaign objectives. Furthermore, one can target specific audiences, and adjust bids according to the audience value to the particular advertiser. With media strategy in place, a DSP can bid with an optimal CPM for each impression in real time, taking into account everything it knows about the impression.

With the rise of automated buying using DSPs, more specialists are needed to develop and execute campaign strategies. On the other hand, fewer people will be necessary in handling media buying transactions. DSPs increasingly work directly with advertisers, bypassing traditional media agencies. This leads to the already mentioned shift of programmatic know-how in-house, particularly when it comes to big advertisers.

Some DSPs are gradually leaving a pure play model, acquiring SSP (supply side platform) or DMP (data management platform) capabilities. This process goes both ways, with SSPs invading traditional DSP territory as well. While it makes competitive sense to widen the ad tech stacks, this merging makes it less clear whether a particular platform stands on the publisher or the advertiser side.

There is a large number of DSPs to choose from at the moment, each with specific strengths and weaknesses. Some of the better known players include DataXu, AOL, Turn, The Trade Desk, MediaMath, Google's Doubleclick Bid Manager (DBM), Rocket Fuel, AudienceScience, Appnexus or Adform.

Agency trading desks

Agency trading desks (ATDs) are specialized programmatic media buying units within large media agencies or agency holding companies. They often handle all programmatic activities for clients, typically using one or multiple standard DSPs – or even bespoke bidder solutions. Some of the well-known ATDs include Xaxis (WPP Group), Accuen (Omnicom Media Group) or Cadreon (IPG Mediabrands).

The concept of agency trading desks, while successful in the past, is facing challenges. Many large clients are moving their programmatic operations in-house – not only in hopes of lower costs, but also to gain more control and transparency over their media buying process. Furthermore, in-house programmatic operations enable data collection, better insight, and more sophisticated communication strategies, while growing internal know-how. Some advertisers also choose to employ

Independent trading desks instead of ATDs.

The ATD model continues to evolve though, to better face technology changes, market pressures from DSPs and other players, as well as client needs and concerns. For example VivaKi (the former Publicis ATD) has been transformed into a technology development and support unit, while letting other agencies within the group handle programmatic media buying[i]. Others, like Xaxis or Accuen, are starting to position themselves not as ATDs, but rather as independent programmatic media companies[ii].

Publishers

On the sell side, publishers are key players in the programmatic ecosystem – because they control digital content and related ad inventory. Publishers range from the premium, well-known media brands to long-tail one-person blogs. They vary not only in scale, but also in the content and inventory formats they offer, as well as audiences they attract. While some publishers have been around for decades, many are products of the digital era. Programmatic advertising marks a new chapter in the ad trading history, bringing digital publishers many new challenges and opportunities.

Traditionally, big publishers sold their digital inventory through an in-house direct sales team, which negotiated inventory deals with advertisers or their agencies. With the advent of ad networks and ad exchanges, the non-premium and remnant inventory was gradually offered via non-direct channels. Programmatic advertising poses the greatest challenge to traditional direct sales models to date, as barriers to offering even the most premium inventory in an automated fashion gradually disappear. With new technologies such as header bidding, publishers can dynamically allocate inventory between direct and programmatic campaigns, increasing effective scale and attractiveness of biddable premium inventory.

Ultimately, with fewer sales and ad trafficking staff required, automation can bring lower costs to the publishers. On the other hand, technology and talent investment to facilitate this transition can be significant. However, even with a greater shift to programmatic, the in-house direct sales are not likely to disappear completely. Their focus will probably move to the most premium inventory, custom campaigns, and new trading models – such as automated guaranteed.

Perhaps the greatest opportunity programmatic era brought to publishers is the widespread use of data to inform inventory buying decisions. Many publishers sit on valuable, large scale data that can be collected, utilized and monetized via a data management platform. Data benefits publishers in several ways, including direct data sales, increased inventory value or user-level content customization.

First of all, publishers can create behavioral and other audience segments which can be sold directly for ad targeting as third-party data. Publisher third-party data can be of high quality and very valuable (for example top-level managers or new car intenders), and utilized either within publisher inventory, or elsewhere. Secondly, the use of data in general by advertisers can increase inventory yield by making some of the individual impressions much more valuable. If an advertiser knows that a particular ad will be displayed to someone who has shown interest in their product category, they are likely to bid more for the impression. The cumulative effect of data usage on publisher revenue can be significant. Last but not least, publishers can use their data collected via a DMP to customize content for individual visitors. This way, a sports buff will see a different homepage to a fashion-conscious teenager, increasing relevance and improving user experience.

As new ad formats and channels become available for trading through programmatic channels, publishers can benefit from enabling and extending their inventory. Current growth of programmatic digital video along with rich media formats is a good example, and publishers who embrace these trends will reap the rewards.

As exciting as the programmatic era is for publishers, they are not without their share of headaches. Not necessarily related to automation, they have to deal with many new trends and technologies which could threaten existing business models. For example, as users give more of their attention to mobile devices, publishers need to solve mobile content monetization and cross-device tracking challenges. Adblocking is a serious concern for many publishers, who could potentially lose a significant portion of their revenues. Also, industry concerns about issues such as ad fraud, viewability, or privacy are likely to significantly alter status quo in the marketplace. To better face these and other challenges, many publishers have chosen to cooperate.

Publisher Co-ops

Pioneered in 2012 by La Place Media in France[iii], publisher co-ops have proven to be a viable and effective business model for premium publishers, particularly in smaller markets. La Place Media was quickly followed by Audience Square, and soon similar initiatives emerged in Denmark (DPN) or the Czech Republic (CPEx). Today, more than ten publisher co-ops exist, in countries as diverse as the UK (AOP and Pangaea), Canada (CPAX), Israel (ILX), Hungary (HOPPex), Greece and Romania (Project Agora), South Africa (SouthernX), Australia (Apex) or New Zealand (KPEX).

The rise of publisher co-ops is fuelled by several key factors. First of all, publishers understand that programmatic technologies will revolutionize the way digital ad inventory is traded. To stay ahead of the curve, they need to significantly invest both financial and human resources to adjust to this new market reality. In smaller markets, where programmatic yield is still low in absolute terms, it makes sense for publishers to share the costs and the know-how. By concentrating their programmatic efforts in a co-op, publishers are able to achieve and afford a level of sophistication they could never hope to attain individually.

Another key factor is scale, and consequently market power. Premium publisher co-ops in smaller markets can achieve the reach and the inventory size to effectively challenge global advertising giants like Google and Facebook. They can offer advertisers the benefits of premium and brand-safe inventory, while retaining full control over access. Publisher co-ops can also serve as catalysts of programmatic advertising market growth. This happened in the Czech Republic for instance, where the CPEx alliance unlocked vast new supply of premium inventory, previously unavailable via automated channels[iv].

Last but not least, co-ops enable pooling of data across publishers to create more extensive, richer datasets. With a shared data management platform (DMP), publishers can offer advertisers high-quality third-party behavioral data with a significant reach. This is critical, as targeting data availability coupled with premium inventory enables local publishers to compete on par with data-rich global players.

Continued growth of publisher co-ops both in numbers and size is a welcome development for the programmatic advertising ecosystem. They offer an alternative to publishers against big ad networks and closed advertising systems, creating a more balanced and healthy market. At the same time, publisher co-ops increase market sophistication and data availability, setting themselves up for a key role in the future shape of programmatic ad trading.

Supply side platforms

A supply side platform (or SSP) makes it possible to sell advertising inventory in a programmatic way. While DSPs are most often used by advertisers and agencies, SSPs are commonly utilized by online publishers. SSPs are designed to maximize yield (aggregate revenue) from publisher inventory, using more or less sophisticated rules and algorithms.

SSPs have the benefit of connecting publisher inventory to a number of demand sources – such as ad exchanges, networks and DSPs. This inventory can then be accessed by a wide range of potential buyers, who compete against each other for available impressions. A good SSP ensures that each impression has a chance to sell for the maximum price the market is willing to pay at that particular point in time – whether through a real-time auction, direct deal, or other transaction method.

Apart from connecting publishers to programmatic ecosystem, SSPs grant them a great deal of control over their inventory. Publishers can decide not only who can buy what inventory through which channels, but also what is the minimum price the inventory can be purchased for. This is accomplished by setting price floors and demand or inventory rules – options and flexibility depends on a particular SSP. For instance, a publisher might decide to completely block a particular advertiser, or only allow purchase of particular inventory if the bid is very high.

Publishers can use supply side platforms to both open up their inventory to the market in open RTB, as well as to traffic specific advertiser deals agreed by their direct sales teams. SSPs enable setup of very detailed advertiser deals, which can include variables such as price floor, inventory, formats, permitted DSPs, and even selected audience segments at which the campaign is to be targeted. Moreover, a deal can include "first look", letting the advertiser buy impressions falling within the deal before anyone else. This option usually carries a premium price though.

Each deal has its own "Deal ID", a short unique alphanumeric string generated by SSP. The Deal ID is given to the advertiser/agency, and allows them to target a particular deal in their DSP. This is not without problems though – Deal IDs are typically sent via e-mail or in a spreadsheet, and the set-up process is prone to errors. Some SSPs are therefore developing new ways of setting up deals, avoiding the explicit use of a Deal ID. The Deal ID and its applications will be discussed in more detail further on.

SSPs also allow publishers to create private market-places (PMPs), something between an open market-place and direct deals. The PMP is only available to selected advertisers, who typically benefit from access to more premium (and brand safe) inventory, first look, increased transparency and less competitive auction. PMP deals are more expensive and need to be negotiated between the publisher and each advertiser. PMPs are usually accessed using a Deal ID.

Just like many DSPs, some SSPs are gradually expanding their offering to include bidding functionality and other technologies. The line between SSPs, DSPs, DMPs and other ad tech vendor types is becoming blurrier. Some of the well known supply side platforms are Rubicon Project, AppNexus, PubMatic, OpenX, AOL or Google's AdX.

Data management platforms

Data management platform (DMP) is a fairly complex piece of software used to collect, store, classify, analyze and manage large quantities of data from various sources, making it useful and actionable particularly in the marketing process. A DMP can typically take in data from a large number of disparate sources, including CRM systems, websites, apps, or external partners.

DMPs can be standalone (such as Adobe Audience Manager) or integrated (Google Doubleclick Audience Center). Standalone data management platforms can be plugged into any DSP, but data loss in synchronization poses a common problem. Integrated DMP can be easier to manage, but are typically tied to a particular advertising platform. For some marketers, a simple DMP functionality built right into a DSP (offered for example by Adform) might be an interesting option.

DMPs are used differently by publishers, marketers, and agencies. For publishers, a DMP serves to augment inventory with data to make it more valuable. A common use case is creating audience segments based on data collected on their visitors (such as "Travel intenders" or "Avid photographers"). Audience segments can then be used to target individual users with relevant online advertising in prospecting campaigns. This is achieved by plugging data from a DMP into a DSP (as a part of a private deal, or through direct integration) – the DSP will then bid only on the impressions aimed at the correct audience. Augmenting impressions with data makes them much more valuable to advertisers, increasing the value of publishers' inventory.

Audience segments can be created either manually, or automatically. Manual segmentation involves an analyst selecting the relevant data and creating a segment definition. An example of automatic segment creation is Look-a-like modeling. In this case, a base user characteristic is selected (such as visitors of a particular site, or users belonging to a specific audience segment), and an algorithm automatically looks for similar users across the entire database. Look-a-like modelling is very useful for instance in prospecting campaigns, allowing advertisers to reach out to potential customers who are similar to visitors to their website (or to existing customers). More on Look-a-like modelling is in chapter four.

DMPs are also useful for agencies and marketers. Agencies can use DMPs to manage data from client campaigns, often creating valuable datasets in the process. For marketers, DMPs can make data actionable across a wide range of channels (unlike CRM systems, which tend to be used only for emailing). At the same time, data management platforms allow marketers to take control of their data, which might be extremely valuable or sensitive.

Some of the big DMP vendors include Adobe (Audience Manager), Oracle (BlueKai), Nielsen (eXelate), Krux, or Lotame.

Industry bodies

Interactive Advertising Bureau

The Interactive Advertising Bureau (IAB)[v] is a trade organization with over 650 members, including media and technology companies in the digital advertising space. The IAB is particularly influential in the United States (where it represents around 86 percent of online advertising) and Europe, but is functioning globally. It was founded in 1996, and is headquartered in New York city.

Interactive Advertising Bureau leads the industry in a number of areas, and is key for programmatic advertising growth. It facilitates development of important standards, such as OpenRTB or OpenDirect, enabling programmatic ad trading among many diverse market players. The IAB also conducts research, and publishes white papers, guidelines and best practices on a wide range of industry topics. Member education is key, and the IAB offers a range of seminars, classes, training programs and even a professional certification. There is a plethora of events organized or supported by the IAB, from council and committee meetings to major industry conferences.

The IAB is also very active when it comes to public policy, where it represents the interests of its members and the digital industry. It strives to promote self-regulation, and shape legislation in a way that enables digital advertising growth and development.

Trustworthy Accountability Group

The Trustworthy Accountability Group[vi] (TAG) is is a joint project created by the IAB, American Association of Advertising Agencies (4A's) and Association of National Advertisers (ANA). TAG aims to increase transparency and accountability across the digital ad industry, focusing on eliminating fraudulent traffic, combating malware, combating ad-supported internet piracy and promoting brand safety.

Media Rating Council

The Media Rating Council's[vii] objective is to secure valid, reliable and effective audience measurement services for the media industry and related users. It also aims to evolve and determine minimum disclosure and ethical criteria for media audience measurement services, and to provide and administer an audit system designed to inform users as to whether such audience measurements are conducted in conformance with the criteria and procedures developed. The Council seeks to improve quality of audience measurement by rating services and to provide a better understanding of the applications and limitations of rating information. For example, the MRC is responsible for setting the display advertising viewability standards used within the programmatic ecosystem.

Other industry bodies and regulators

There are of course other industry organizations contributing to development, standardization and self-regulation of programmatic advertising. These include for example the aforementioned American Association of Advertising Agencies (4A's) and Association of National Advertisers (ANA), as well as the Digital Advertising Alliance (DAA) or Direct Marketing Association (DMA). Naturally, similar bodies exist in many countries across the globe.

Government influence and regulation plays a key role as well. The Federal Trade Commission[viii] (FTC) is particularly important in the US, while the European Commission strives to regulate the European market. National laws further regulate programmatic and other forms of advertising on a country level.

Specialized industry vendors

Vendors providing specialized services further enrich the programmatic ecosystem. These include third-party data vendors (such as Experian or Acxiom), who collect, package and resell data useful for ad targeting and other applications. Third-party data will be covered in more detail later in this book.

There are also specialized retargeting vendors, helping advertisers get the most out of their first-party data. Retargeting (including retargeting vendors) is covered later in more detail.

With the increasing awareness of fraud and viewability issues, new vendors have sprung up to address them. They help advertisers (and to some extent publishers too) to determine whether an ad was shown to a human, and if so, whether he or she had a chance to actually see it. Separate sections will cover both fraud and viewability in depth.

3 PROGRAMMATIC TRADING

Now that we introduced programmatic ecosystem play-ers, let's look at how they interact. In this chapter, we will discuss several common ways in which program-matic transactions can be executed, and their respective benefits and downsides. We will explore both auction-based, as well as fixed price transactions, and the under-lying OpenRTB and OpenDirect protocols which ena-ble them.

A separate section of chapter three is dedicated to real-time bidding auction, as knowledge of the general mechanics is indispensable for running successful auction-based programmatic campaigns. To round out this overview of programmatic trading, we will look at the role of the deal ID in more detail, as well as publisher prioritization including header bidding.

Programmatic transaction types

Programmatic advertising currently encompasses four basic transaction types – open auction, invitation-only auction, unreserved fixed rate and automated guaranteed[ix]. These transaction types are differentiated by two main factors – whether an auction is involved in determining inventory price, and whether the inventory is reserved or not. A common misconception equates auction-based transaction types (commonly referred to as RTB, or real-time bidding) with programmatic advertising, ignoring fixed-price transaction types.

Programmatic transaction types

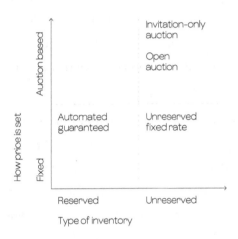

Source: Interactive Advertising Bureau 2013

Open vs. invitation-only auction

If an auction is involved in setting inventory price, we talk about either open auction, or invitation-only auction. In both cases, inventory is unreserved, and real-time bidding technology underlies ad inventory buying. Open auction (also known as open marketplace or open exchange) is by far the most prevalent program-matic transaction type[x], and is generally accessible to all buyers. Publishers can still restrict access to some buyers via blocklists or individual inventory price floors though. To protect direct sales and other more premium channels, publishers often mask urls in an open auction (multiple domains are grouped under the same url), or the auction is completely blind (url is not disclosed at all).

Unlike an open auction, invitation-only auction (private marketplace, or PMP) is exclusive to a limited number of advertisers selected by the publisher. To make this auction format attractive, publishers can for instance offer transparent urls, access to more premium inventory, exclusive data, or give first look (auction priority) to some advertisers.

Automated guaranteed and unreserved fixed rate

In case the inventory price is fixed and no auction takes place, we can distinguish either unreserved fixed rate, or automated guaranteed. With unreserved fixed rate, there is no inventory set aside specifically for the advertiser, but the price is fixed. Such deals sometimes have a priority over auction-type transactions, in order to ensure campaign delivery.

With automated guaranteed, also known as programmatic direct or programmatic premium, the price is fixed and the inventory is guaranteed. Automated guaranteed is similar to traditional direct sales, but with the advantage of automation. Such deals are typically negotiated and agreed by publishers' sales teams, and trafficked programmatically alongside other transaction types. With automated guaranteed, unlike auction-based transaction types, advertisers typically cannot pick individual impressions they might be more interested in.

Automating the direct sales process can mean significant time savings on both buy and sell sides. With simpler workflow, fewer ad operations staff are needed to traffic and manage digital campaigns. There's also a lower risk of human error, or unnecessary set up delays. Compared to auction-based transaction types, automated guaranteed offers advertisers an assurance that their campaign will achieve required impression volume. Other benefits, such as the option to use data for targeting, are shared with other programmatic transaction types.

OpenRTB and OpenDirect

In order to simplify communication between buyers and suppliers of inventory in the programmatic ecosystem, protocol standards have been developed to support all of the basic transaction types. OpenRTB, originally started in 2010 as a pilot project between a handful of DSPs and SSPs, has now been adopted as an IAB standard. The OpenRTB protocol is maintained and continuously improved by the RTB Project, a working group within IAB Technology Council. Existing separately alongside OpenRTB, OpenDirect is a standard for buying and selling automated guaranteed ad inventory. The aim of these protocols is not only to simplify communication, but also to enable greater innovation and growth within programmatic.

OpenRTB API specification is a very detailed guide to the RTB interface. It describes basic interactions taking place between an exchange and bidders, including bid requests, bid responses, win notices and ad markups. Each interaction must follow a prescribed format and contain a number of attributes – some of which are required, and others recommended or optional. For example, a bid request must contain information such as unique auction ID, one or several impression IDs and impression type (banner, video or native) for each impression offered. Other attributes of the bid request can include site (or app), device and user information, or the minimum bid.

In addition to describing the content and the structure of basic RTB interactions, OpenRTB protocol suggests JSON as the ideal data format. As for video, OpenRTB protocol assumes compliance with VAST standard. Additional, more granular specifications also fall under this standard, such as Native Ad Specification. While fairly prescriptive, OpenRTB protocol still leaves room for customization – for instance, exchanges can offer additional data formats, or exchange specific extensions to the standard. The full specification can be downloaded from IAB website[xi].

Real-time bidding auction

Given that auction-based transaction types currently make up the bulk of programmatic advertising, it is very useful to understand how a real-time bidding auction works.

An auction enables buying and selling of individual ad impressions in a fraction of a second, letting all participants trade each impression at its current market price. Every real-time bidding auction follows a process established by the OpenRTB protocol. An auction happens in real time (while the user is waiting for a page to load), and typically takes less than 100 milliseconds. A separate auction is usually held for each available impression on the page. The auction proceeds in the following eight steps:

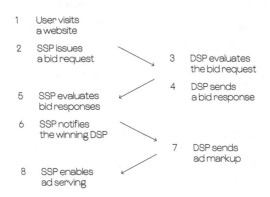

Real-time bidding auction

1	User visits a website		
2	SSP issues a bid request	3	DSP evaluates the bid request
		4	DSP sends a bid response
5	SSP evaluates bid responses		
6	SSP notifies the winning DSP		
		7	DSP sends ad markup
8	SSP enables ad serving		

1) *User visits a website*

When a user visits a publisher website, their browser requests content from various sources in order to render the page. Some of the content will come directly from publisher servers (usually main content, such as an article or a video the user came to see). Ads, however, might come from elsewhere, particularly with an RTB auction. In a real-time bidding auction, the request to fill an available ad slot typically goes from a publisher page to a publisher ad server, which (under pre-defined conditions) redirects the request to a Supply-side platform.

2) *Supply-side platform issues a bid request*

SSP handles the auction for an available impression on behalf of a publisher. It issues a bid request to all Demand-side platforms which might participate in the auction. The bid request contains information which can be useful to the participating parties in making an informed decision about a bid. As noted previously, OpenRTB protocol defines which parameters are required, recommended or optional in a bid request. A bid request can also contain data related to the user who is about to see an ad, making the impression potentially more valuable to some advertisers.

3) Demand-side platform evaluates the bid request

Upon receiving the bid request, a DSP will determine how valuable the impression is, and whether to participate in the auction. A number of factors can play a role – such as publisher, placement, floor price, user value or constraints like frequency caps or budget limits.

4) Demand-side platform sends a bid response

If a DSP decides to participate in the auction (i.e. the bid request falls within the rules set up in the DSP for a particular campaign), it will issue a bid response. Just like a bid request, the bid response has a specific format outlined in the OpenRTB protocol. A bid response contains one or several bids from various seats (i.e. buyers, usually different advertisers or agencies) under the same DSP, or even from the same seat (one advertiser/agency with several campaigns). A bid response usually includes Ad Markup (Ad Tag or Ad serving code, so the ad can be rendered).

5) Supply-side platform evaluates bid responses

The SSP gathers all bid responses from participating DSPs, and picks a winner under the auction rules. The impression is usually awarded to the highest bidder (at a price slightly above the second highest bid, so called second-price auction). However, other criteria might come into play – some advertisers could be blocked by the publisher for instance, so they cannot win the auction.

6) Supply-side platform notifies the winning DSP

The SSP sends a win notice to the winning DSP, which includes the settlement price. Loss notice is not issued in the real time to other participants (but lost bid data can be shared later in a separate process).

7) Demand-side platform sends Ad Markup

In case the DSP didn't already send Ad Markup in a bid response, it must be sent at this point. Ad Markup is normally sent in a bid response though.

8) Supply-side platform enables ad serving

Concluding the real-time bidding auction, SSP passes Ad Markup of the winning bidder along to a user's browser. Ad is then served, together with other content on the web page. All of these steps happen so fast that users can't even notice an auction happening in the background, while a page is loading.

Deal ID

The Deal ID[xii] is a unique identifier designed to help buyers and sellers set up custom programmatic deals. When advertisers and publishers negotiate a deal (regardless of the actual transaction type), they can for instance agree a certain price floor (or fixed price), inventory, targeting, priority, or url transparency.

When a deal is set up in the SSP, a unique Deal ID is generated to identify it. The Deal ID becomes another attribute of the bid request, signifying that all of the bid requests containing this Deal ID are only for impressions with agreed parameters. The Deal ID is then sent over (usually via e-mail) to an advertiser or their agency, and assigned to a line item in the DSP. This way, DSPs and SSPs know that a particular bid request or response is related to a specific deal, and behave accordingly.

Prioritization and header bidding

Publishers have many options when it comes to monetizing their inventory in the open programmatic ecosystem. They can opt for a pure real-time bidding/programmatic model, or a combination with other sources of demand. More advanced publishers commonly use a built-in ad server to manage their inventory, sometimes with an integrated SSP. Large publishers take it a step further, and utilize more or less complex waterfall setups, or the increasingly popular header bidding.

With a waterfall setup, publishers usually fill available impressions through demand from various sources in a decreasing order of priority. Direct campaigns typically have the highest priority, whether programmatic or not. If an impression is not filled by a direct campaign, it is usually offered in a private and subsequently open auction.

Each publisher can have a different default priority order, with lots of options for individual tweaks on a deal/campaign basis. Deals can for instance include first-look, giving a selected advertiser the option to purchase impressions ahead of anyone else. However complex though, waterfall setups are created manually based on historical data and business considerations. This leads to sub-optimal overall yield for publishers, and restricted inventory access for advertisers.

The problem might be solved by header bidding, which has been generating a lot of buzz recently. In essence, header bidding technology enables a publisher to solicit bids for each impression from multiple demand sources simultaneously, rather than sequentially. This gives every demand source potentially equal inventory access, and the increased competition for each impression translates into higher effective CPM and overall publisher revenue.

Exact implementation of header bidding will vary by publisher and specific circumstances, but the technology is always based on a JavaScript tag placed in the header section of a website (hence the name). This piece of code initiates a preliminary auction, inviting integrated partners to submit actual bids for the offered inventory. Armed with real-time impression value information, a publisher can then dynamically prioritize demand sources (such as directly sold campaigns, demand from SSPs, or retargeters) to maximize yield.

Main benefit to publishers is increased competition for each individual impression, driving up winning bids and overall inventory value. Publishers still retain control over auction participants, and their prioritization beyond the highest bid. For example, a publisher can still choose to award an impression to a participant who didn't submit the highest bid, if other considerations (such as a contractual agreement) warrant this. Advertisers benefit from header bidding as well, as they gain potential access to the entire publisher inventory. They can also make better use of their data, and even enhance it in the process[xiii].

Header bidding is not entirely without issues. Since a JavaScript tag is implemented in the website header, some publishers might be worried about slow page loading. Header bidding is typically implemented asynchronously though, so as to avoid page latency. Another issue is a limit on the number of demand sources publishers choose to integrate into the header auction. Other demand sources can participate indirectly through one of the integrated ones, but typically need to pay transaction fees which puts them at a disadvantage[xiv]. This can lead to market consolidation and decreased competition.

Despite these issues, header bidding is quickly becoming the new standard in publisher inventory management. This is good news for programmatic advertising, as better inventory access will allow more and more digital campaigns to be traded in an automated fashion.

4 DATA

Data is the lifeblood of programmatic advertising. While automation makes ad buying more efficient, it is data that elevates programmatic to its game-changer status. Advertisers can know their customers and prospects like never before, and use this information within the programmatic ecosystem to individually tailor communication at an unprecedented scale. This is a true marketing revolution, and data is front and center.

Data comes in many guises. The most common (and the focus of this chapter) is audience data. Other interesting data types exist as well though, including location (more on this in chapter five) or weather data. Event-based data (such as sports-related events, e.g. scoring a point or winning a game) can be also very useful – particularly if utilized in real-time. As will be discussed later in this chapter, impression context (if determined accurately) is also a handy data point when it comes to ad targeting.

To kick off this chapter, we will look at basic data categorization based on source (first-, second- or third-party) and collection method (declared, inferred or modelled). These classifications are commonly used across the industry, and it's very useful to have a firm grasp of their meaning.

Since the most common use of data within the programmatic ecosystem is ad targeting, the majority of this chapter is dedicated to various targeting options. Retargeting is perhaps best known (and somewhat overused) tactic, and we'll look at both the basic retargeting process as well as more advanced options and implementations.

Beyond retargeting, this chapter will present a number of targeting tactics that fall under the broad umbrella of prospecting. These include contextual targeting, behavioral targeting and look-a-like modelling. Finally, we'll briefly touch upon some of the ways which enable data usage within the programmatic ecosystem, including cookie synching and role of the Deal ID.

Data categorization

First-party data

One common data categorization based on source is into the first, second, and third-party. First-party data is collected directly from your own users. This is the most valuable, exclusive and accurate data marketers have (and it's free!). For example, an e-commerce site can collect data on its visitors, including products they viewed, put into a shopping basket, or purchased. From this data, they can determine purchase intent or other behavioral patterns, and personalize their marketing approach for each visitor. Retargeting, which will be discussed later, is the most common use of first-party data.

As great as first-party data is, limited scale is a major downside. In order for the e-commerce site to obtain such data, users must first visit their website. Only a fraction of their potential customers do so, so other methods have to be used to reach out to the rest. First-party data use can be also limited due to legal reasons. It has to be handled and used in line with privacy laws, as well as any user agreements that were made at the time of data collection.

Second-party data

Second-party data is obtained through partnerships with other entities, and is basically their first-party data. To illustrate, a price comparison site might share their first-party customer data with an e-commerce site. To the e-commerce site, this is second-party data – and is indeed very valuable. Often, partners would mutually share their first-party data in order to gain a better user understanding, or to extend their cross-device ID recognition. Second-party data sharing can also take the form of data co-ops, where multiple partners (typically publishers) pool their data together.

Given the high quality and uniqueness of second-party data, demand for it is picking up. To many data owners, such as small specialized publishers, providing their valuable data to close partners can open up a new revenue stream. A downside for all parties is the need to maintain data-sharing partnerships, and potential data leaks if partners are unreliable. Data rights and privacy issues are even more critical when providing data to other parties. First-party data often can't be shared unless user consent to do so is obtained in advance.

Third-party data

Finally, third-party data is data obtained from external providers, with no direct partnership with the buyer. For example, a publisher data sharing co-op can segment visitors based on their browsing behavior, and sell these segments to advertisers for campaign targeting. To the advertiser, these segments (say car purchase intenders or photography buffs) constitute third-party data. Such data can be very useful in efficiently extending advertising campaigns to wider audiences of potential customers.

Third-party data is widely used, mainly for ad targeting. Some of the advantages include easy access, large scale, and increased return on advertising investment. Demand-side platforms typically offer a wide selection of integrated audience segments from a number of providers, which can be easily added to any campaign. Some vendors have access to both vast as well as high quality data sources, offering advertisers scale they wouldn't be able to achieve with just first- and second-party data. Finally, third-party data use frequently shows high ROI, especially when a campaign is based around the right segments of sufficient quality.

However, not all third-party data is created equal, and advertisers need to be very careful when evaluating data vendors. Data quality can vary greatly, as each provider is free to collect and package data in their own way. Transparency is often limited when it comes to third-party data, so factors such as trust and previous experience with vendors come into play. Many third-party data providers are available, from publishers and publisher co-ops to specialist vendors such as Experian, Acxiom, Lotame, Oracle (BlueKai) and others.

Declared, inferred and modelled data

Depending on how data was collected, it can be classified as declared, inferred or modelled. Declared data is given by the users themselves, and might include things such as age, gender, interests and so on. Facebook is a treasure trove of declared data, from user profiles to things they like or share. Declared data is commonly collected from registration forms, or by running sweepstakes. Inferred data is not given by the users directly, but is deduced – usually from their behavior. Someone reading a lot of computer game reviews is likely to be interested in playing computer games. Finally, modelled data uses a large data set to find users matching a desired profile. Typical application is look-a-like modelling, where an algorithm tries to find users who are similar to a given user group.

Retargeting

Retargeting is a form of behavioral targeting aimed at users an advertiser already knows, typically through first-party data. Although retargeting technically falls under behavioral targeting, it deserves a separate section given its importance and specific role in current display advertising strategies. There is little doubt that retargeting is very effective, so much so that it has become somewhat of a mandatory item in any media plan. After all, what could possibly work better than communicating with people who have already in some way (usually by visiting your website) shown interest in your brand or product?

Retargeting process

Retargeting can be fairly simple, but it can also become a fairly complex endeavor. Before discussing it further, it is helpful to understand the process of simple site retargeting using an external retargeting vendor. Let's suppose an e-commerce advertiser wants to show their ads to users who put an item into a shopping basket, but didn't complete a purchase. This is how the magic happens:

Retargeting

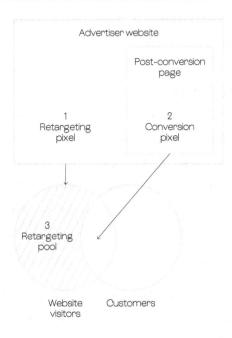

1. Retargeting pixel from a chosen vendor is placed on an advertiser's website. This can include an entire website, or just selected pages (for example the basket page in case of an e-commerce site).

2. Conversion pixel from the vendor is placed on a post-conversion page, to track users who have already converted. This can be a "thank you for your purchase"

page for instance. This pixel is there to ensure that visitors, who have already converted, are excluded from the retargeting campaign.

3. When a user visits advertiser's website, the retargeting pixel saves a cookie into their browser. All of the users who have a cookie set (and possibly meet other criteria, such as no conversion in the last month) form a retargeting pool.

4. The vendor needs to use cookie synching or other form of data transfer with its partners (such as Ad Exchanges), in order to be able to recognize bid requests related to users in the retargeting pool. How cookie synching works is discussed towards the end of this chapter.

5. Retargeting vendor bids on selected requests related to users in the retargeting pool. Bidding algorithms differ with each vendor, and vary in their degree of sophistication. The vendor aims to win as many impressions as possible while maintaining high efficiency.

6. As users in a retargeting pool browse the web, they see ads the retargeting vendor has purchased on behalf of an advertiser. If they make a conversion (for example a purchase) on an advertiser's website, they are usually excluded from the retargeting pool for some time.

Spicing things up

This is site retargeting process in a nutshell. However, there is a lot of freedom and flexibility in how it can be set up. An advertiser can define their retargeting pool in any way, particularly if they have access to a Data Management Platform. There's no reason to use just one retargeting pool, either. An advertiser can run a separate retargeting campaign for regular customers who haven't made a purchase in a while, and for new ones who showed interest (perhaps by making more than five page views on the site, or putting something in a shopping basket), but didn't proceed to click the buy button. Also, there is no set optimal frequency for retargeting campaigns, and it should be adjusted for each retargeting pool to achieve an optimal return – without alienating potential customers.

Dynamic retargeting is also a very common way to improve retargeting efficiency. Rather than showing the same creative to all users in the retargeting pool, the creative is personalized based on what exactly each user viewed on the advertiser's site. For example, if a user viewed a specific camera (say Fujifilm X100T) on an e-commerce site, a vendor employing dynamic retargeting would put together a creative featuring Fujifilm X100T on the fly, in response to a bid request for this particular user. Creative is personalized automatically based on a product feed supplied by the advertiser, for all users and all impressions which are part of the dynamic retargeting campaign. The product feed contains data such as product names or images, and is commonly supplied in an .xml, .csv or .txt format.

Beyond site retargeting

So far we have only discussed site retargeting, but other forms of retargeting exist as well, including e-mail retargeting, search retargeting, and e-mail list retargeting. With simple e-mail retargeting, ads are shown to users who have opened an advertiser's e-mail. Search retargeting is a tactic where users who have searched for selected keywords are retargeted.

Increasingly popular is retargeting using e-mail lists (sometimes referred to as CRM retargeting). An advertiser simply uploads an e-mail list from their database to a vendor, who matches the e-mail addresses to user cookies (with varying match rates depending on the vendor). These users can then be retargeted as if they had visited the advertiser site. E-mail list retargeting is common on Facebook and Twitter, where other user credentials beyond e-mail address (such as a phone number or social network ID) can be used to create a custom retargeting audience. Google has recently introduced a very powerful and exciting e-mail list retargeting product as well, called AdWords Customer Match. Retargeting pools can be used directly within Google AdWords, bringing potential efficiency to a whole new level.

As users spend increasingly more time on mobile devices, and often use them to complete purchases, mobile retargeting is gaining in importance. While desktop retargeting is based largely on cookies, these are not widely available on mobile devices. Other means of identification in addition to cookies are used to accomplish the task, such as Apple's Identifier for Advertisers (IDFA) on iOS, Google's Identifier for Advertisers (AAID) on Android or the Facebook ID in the Facebook ecosystem (including the site itself, as well as apps using Facebook SDK). With the rise of cross-device solutions, desktop and mobile retargeting will continue to converge. The next chapter will delve deeper into specific topics related to mobile.

Retargeting vendors

There is a large number of specialized retargeting vendors to choose from, including AdRoll, Retargeter, Criteo or Sociomantic. Advertisers can also implement retargeting using their DSP, or platforms like Twitter or

Facebook. Vendors differ in the scope and the quality of their inventory partnerships (only some vendors have access to Facebook Exchange for instance), retargeting setup options, and the sophistication of bidding algorithms, among other factors.

It is a good idea for an advertiser to centralize retargeting, and to use a single vendor. Otherwise, with multiple vendors running retargeting campaigns simultaneously on the same retargeting pools, auction prices will inevitably (and unnecessarily) increase. At the same time, users will be targeted with very high frequencies, combining frequency caps of all participating retargeting vendors. This leads to lower overall efficiency and might even alienate potential customers.

Retargeting vs. prospecting

It is good to make an important distinction at this point. As noted previously, retargeting means reaching out to users (or cookies) the advertiser already knows and who have shown strong interest or purchase intent, typically because they already visited their website. Retargeting is the most prevalent use of first-party data. As an advertising tactic, retargeting is very effective, but limited in scale (vast majority of potential customers are not known to the advertiser yet).

Prospecting, on the other hand, means looking for potential customers an advertiser doesn't know yet, with the aim of bringing them to a retargeting pool and ultimately up the marketing funnel. This is where second- and third-party data comes into play in the programmatic ecosystem. Let's say a baby product retailer wants to grow its customer base. A sound strategy is to attract potential new shoppers through a prospecting campaign aimed at relevant audience segments (such as mothers of babies). Once such prospects show interest and visit the retailer's website, they can be communicated with very efficiently through retargeting. A good media planner (whether in-house or at an agency) should be able to combine the right prospecting and retargeting tactics, to achieve optimal return on investment.

It is important to distinguish between retargeting and prospecting tactics when looking at attribution (there is a dedicated section in chapter six). Partly due to the prevalence of Google Analytics as advertisers' primary analytics platform for evaluating campaigns, last-click (or last-impression) attribution is often used to compare effectiveness of different campaigns, channels or tactics. Unfortunately, this leads to undervaluation of prospecting, and overvaluation of retargeting. While prospecting might make a potential customer aware of an advertiser's offer and bring them to the relevant site, they will likely not purchase straight away. This potential customer falls into the retargeting pool, and might eventually convert. With last-click or last-impression attribution model, prospecting will likely get no credit for this conversion, while retargeting gets all of it. The result for an advertiser, if evaluating prospecting and retargeting together based on last-click or last-impression attribution model, is suboptimal budget allocation to the detriment of prospecting (and campaign results overall).

Prospecting

In order to communicate with new potential customers an advertiser doesn't know yet, several prospecting tactics can be incorporated into an overall strategy. In this section, we will explore some of them, including contextual targeting, behavioral targeting, and look-a-like modelling.

Contextual targeting

Website content (or website audience profile, if known) has traditionally been used to target advertising, based on presumed overlap with advertisers' potential customers. For example, if the content of a site is based around childcare, an advertiser can expect to be able to target an audience of mums there. A media planner would select a portfolio of sites where the advertiser's audience could be reached, and their campaign would run there. This method of targeting is still very common online (and of course in the offline media, such as newspapers, magazines or TV). Compared to some other forms of targeting (including behavioral targeting discussed later), content-based targeting has a big advantage in being cookie-free. Over time, content-based targeting has evolved to more sophisticated forms, including contextual targeting and semantic targeting.

Contextual targeting relies on scanning pages for specific keywords, in order to estimate relevance of a page to an advertiser's target group. Keywords or categories are chosen by an advertiser (or their agency), and ads are served on matching pages. This method of targeting is very common, given the relative precision and ease of implementation (many advertisers have fine-tuned keyword lists ready from their PPC campaigns).

There are some drawbacks to contextual targeting though. Firstly, many words have multiple meanings, so a simple scanning technology is unable to determine the exact meaning in the context where they appear. And secondly, basic contextual targeting cannot gauge overall context of a page, including sentiment or appropriateness. Such problems can be partially solved by restricting a keyword list to make it safer, but doing so might limit scale of the campaign. To combat all these drawbacks, semantic targeting has come to the fore in recent years.

Semantic targeting is a more sophisticated form of contextual targeting, utilizing semantic techniques and natural language processing to determine the overall context of a page. Unlike simple contextual targeting, semantic technology is able to recognize the exact meaning of words on a page, as well as content topic and overall sentiment (which can be positive, neutral or negative). Compared to basic contextual targeting, semantic targeting enables larger campaign scale (particularly in bigger markets), while still maintaining relevance and brand safety. Well-known semantic targeting providers include ADmantX or Peer39.

Behavioral targeting

Behavioral targeting, also known as audience targeting, relies on individual user web-browsing behavioral data to increase advertising relevance. For example, if a user started frequently visiting car-related websites to read reviews and compare specs, it is reasonable to assume they are in the market for a new car. It makes sense for a car brand to target advertising to such users, increasing efficiency of their campaigns. In a win-win-win situation, users also benefit from seeing ads they might be interested in, and publishers are able to sell their targeted inventory at higher CPMs.

Behavioral targeting starts by collecting "signals", which are essentially meaningful data points with regard to user intent, interests, or profile. Such signals might include pages visited, keywords users searched for, clicks or other events users triggered, or user-related declared data. Behavioral/audience segments are then defined based on recency and frequency of relevant signals. Various signals can be assigned a different weight – searching for a particular keyword (such as "Ford dealership") could be a stronger indicator of intent than visiting a generic car-related page.

Data management platforms (DMPs) are typically used to facilitate behavioral targeting. Segments are usually defined manually, and the resulting data quality therefore depends not only on the quality of signals, but also on choices made in segment definition. These choices include factors like signal recency, frequency, or strength. For some segments, data quality can be increased through shorter recency windows – this is typically the case with segments capturing purchase intent. Someone searching for "Ford dealership" yesterday is more likely to be in-market than if the search happened a month ago. For other segments, such as those capturing interest, long recency windows along with higher signal frequency requirement might be more appropriate. Another common design choice is the balance of stronger and weaker signals in segment definition – while using only very strong signals improves data quality, it might severely limit scale. Data providers typically aim for a good balance between data quality and scale, which involves a lot of trial and error to get right.

Behavioral targeting is ideal for prospecting campaigns. Advertisers or typically purchase third-party audience data for this purpose, either from specialized data vendors, or directly from publishers. Behavioral data quality varies by data provider, so it always makes sense to test several targeting options. Combined with subsequent retargeting and other parts of a digital communication mix, behavioral targeting is an excellent way to acquire new customers, or spread brand message.

There is some controversy with regard to behavioral targeting, concerning user privacy and data rights. Ideally, such data should be collected only with user consent (or an option to opt out), used only for the agreed purpose, and stored securely and anonymously by a trusted entity. The legal side of things varies by region or country, and so does user awareness and sensitivity. Technology in this space is developing so fast that understanding and legislation concerning behavioral targeting is catching up with some delay, but user privacy protection should always be paramount.

Look-a-like modeling

Look-a-like modeling is an increasingly popular way of using behavioral data, allowing advertisers to achieve both targeting accuracy and scale. It could be classified as a special form of behavioral targeting (just like retargeting), taking advantage of data processing power available today. As noted previously, look-a-like modeling works by algorithmically finding users with similar behaviors or characteristics to a given user group. This process requires a very large user pool, with sufficient amount of data points for each user.

An advertiser usually chooses the audience they would like to extend – base user group. This could be for instance users who have converted on the advertiser's site, site visitors, users belonging to a certain audience segment, or even an e-mail list from a CRM database. The base group must be a subgroup of vendor user pool. Ideally a modeling vendor collects data on the base group directly for subsequent look-a-like modeling. If an advertiser would like to use an external base group (such as an e-mail list from their CRM database), this audience first needs to be matched to the user pool of a vendor. There is usually a minimum base group size for a modeling algorithm to work properly.

Once the base group is selected, an algorithm can look for users who are similar. Resulting quality of a look-a-like model will depend on the vendor algorithm, the quality and the scale of their data (relative to the base group), the size of the base group, and other factors. It is therefore important to choose the right vendor, as results can vary greatly.

There is also typically an inverse correlation between the size of the resulting look-a-like audience and its similarity to the base group. Sometimes the resulting model is either too narrow or too inaccurate to be of any use. However, look-a-like modeling can also work very well, and is a great use of behavioral data to extend campaign reach.

Look-a-like modeling

Vendor user pool

Look-a-like group

Increasing size

Base group

Decreasing relevance

Using data in a DSP

A lot of data used for targeting in programmatic advertising is collected and stored separately from an advertiser's Demand-side platform. This is particularly the case of third-party behavioral data, sold by external data vendors. When the DSP makes a bidding decision, it needs to know that the bid request is for a user (cookie) belonging to a particular audience segment. There are two common ways to achieve this – using cookie synching and via a Deal ID.

Cookie synching

For simplicity, let's assume for now that the DSP knows which cookies set by the DSP belong to a particular audience segment (through an integration with a data provider for example). Also, let's assume that both the SSP and the DSP have already set their cookies in a user's browser. As part of the bid request, the SSP can pass a cookie ID to the DSP. However, the SSP can only read user cookies set under the SSP's domain, and has no access to the cookie set by the DSP. So the SSP cannot directly read and pass the DSP cookie ID. In order for the cookie ID passed by the SSP in a bid request to have any meaning for the DSP, a cookie synch must happen first.

The exact implementation of cookie synching may vary, but a simple example should suffice to illustrate the concept. Here, the SSP will store the cookie ID match table, which is just a database that maps SSP Cookie IDs to DSP Cookie IDs.

This is how the actual synch happens using pixels:

1) User visits a website, where inventory is managed through the SSP. A synchronization pixel will fire, targeted at the DSP domain.

2) Upon receiving the synch request, the DSP reads its cookie ID for the user. It redirects back to the SSP, passing it the DSP's cookie ID.

3) The SSP reads the DSP's cookie ID, and stores it in the match table against its own cookie ID.

4) When the SSP encounters the same user again, it can look up the cookie ID used by the DSP for this user in the match table, and pass it in a bid request. The DSP can analyze what it knows about this user and bid accordingly.

Cookie
synching

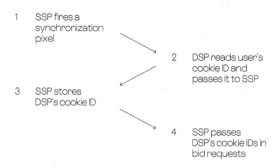

1 SSP fires a
   synchronization
   pixel

2 DSP reads user's
   cookie ID and
   passes it to SSP

3 SSP stores
   DSP's cookie ID

4 SSP passes
   DSP's cookie IDs in
   bid requests

We assumed in the beginning that the DSP already knows which cookies belong to a particular audience segment. This can be because the DSP itself collected the data (typical for retargeting), or because it has an integration with external data vendor. In the latter case, the data vendor and the DSP first need to synchronize their cookies – just like in the above example. Then the data related to individual cookies can be transferred to the DSP either in real-time using pixels, or in regular intervals using batch processing (also referred to as server-to-server integration).

Usage of cookie synching goes beyond the above examples. In fact, it's an underlying technology of the entire programmatic ecosystem, enabling integration between its various players.

Deal ID

The deal ID can also be used to pass the information that a user belongs to a particular audience segment from the SSP to a DSP. In this case, the SSP needs to know that a user belongs to a segment (typically through an integration with a DMP/data vendor). When a deal is set up in the SSP, it can already involve an agreed audience targeting. For example, a deal might only target photography fans or car purchase intenders. The deal is agreed between the SSP, DSP, and the advertiser – so everyone knows which audience segments are included under the deal. All the DSP needs to know is the Deal ID that is passed with a bid request, to make an informed bidding decision. Deal ID is therefore sufficient for the DSP to know that a request is related to a user from a particular audience segment.

5 MOBILE PROGRAMMATIC

As more and more users shift their attention and time to smartphones and tablets, advertisers' budgets are quick to follow. This brings up new challenges for programmatic advertising, as some of the core technologies were originally designed for the desktop environment. Mobile ad tech can for instance no longer rely on third-party cookies, and new approaches are being explored to compensate. Apps dominate mobile device experience, although mobile browsers are still used for many tasks. Advent of mobile means a major shift for programmatic advertising, in terms of inventory, data, and the overall experience.

Mobile browser cookies

Programmatic advertising on desktop is heavily reliant on cookies – from data collection and user targeting to campaign management and reporting. On mobile devices though, cookies (third-party in particular) are not as readily available, and a lot of user activity happens within apps where standard browser cookies don't exist at all. Mobile programmatic needs to look beyond cookies to retain the same functionality and benefits advertisers are used to on desktop. A number of alternatives have been developed, and their combination is often necessary to capture the entire user experience on mobile.

Within most mobile browsers, cookies still exist. First-party cookies can usually be set, but some browsers (most notably Safari on iOS) don't allow third-party cookies. With some browsers, users can also choose to clear their cookies automatically every time they close the browser. Despite these limitations, mobile browser cookies are still useful for programmatic advertising purposes.

Mobile apps are very different to mobile browsers when it comes to storing cookies and data in general[xv]. Each app has its own storage space on a mobile device, so cookies or any other data captured by the app cannot be easily shared between apps (including the mobile browser). However, apps can access a unique ID of a device – Identifier for Advertising (IDFA) on iOS, or Google Advertising ID (AAID) on Android. Device IDs can be used for user identification and tracking, but iOS users are free to reset IDFA or limit its availability for behavioral advertising[xvi].

Apps can take advantage of various SDKs (Software Development Kits), which enable a very detailed data collection of user behavior within an app. SDKs with a wide install base have access to behavioral data across a vast number of apps, effectively replacing cookie-based tracking and targeting. Mobile apps clearly have an upper hand compared to mobile browsers when it comes to user data collection and usage, and it can be expected that publishers will increasingly move their content and inventory inside the app environment.

Cross-device technology (see separate section for an in-depth overview) can also be used to overcome cookie availability limitations on mobile. Deterministic approach in particular, where login is required, effectively eliminates the need for a cookie as an identifier. Moreover, this approach works well across apps and the mobile web. However, only some of the biggest players (such as Facebook, Google, or Twitter) have the scale to take the full advantage of this.

Data on mobile

With the development of cross-device technology and cookie alternatives on mobile, applicability of existing first-, second-, and third-party data is growing. However, mobile devices can supply rich additional data[xvii], ranging from technical (such as device and/or app information) to increasingly valuable geo-location data (see separate section on location-based marketing). Data on mobile, especially if gathered via apps and their SDKs, can be very granular and accurate, providing a more complete and actionable user profile. This has led to a new breed of companies springing up around mobile data, including Apsalar or Flurry.

Mobile inventory

Common mobile programmatic inventory types, available both in mobile web and within apps, include banners, interstitials, video, and native ads[xviii]. Typical banner ad sizes available programmatically on mobile devices are 300x250 and 320x50, but others can be used as well (especially on tablets). The 300x250 format is very prominent on small smartphone screens, and can work well for advertisers. Interstitials are full-page ads which cover the screen, and must be dismissed before a user can return to content (regardless of whether it is an article or a mobile game)[xix].

Mobile video ads can be served either inline in current environment (for example an app or mobile browser), or within a native player on a device. Inline playback can be less disruptive to users, and enables playback metrics reporting[xx].

Mobile native, pioneered by Facebook and Twitter, can be expected to grow even in the open programmatic environment. With a lot of mobile content being served in the form of feeds, native ads are uniquely suited to deliver consistent user experience regardless of publisher. A separate section of this book explores native advertising in more detail.

Despite all these challenges, it is clear that convergence of programmatic ad tech and mobile platforms will continue and accelerate. This will bring new opportunities to advertisers with richer data and potentially more engaging and efficient ad formats. Equally, mobile programmatic can open new revenue streams for publishers, and bring more relevant and less disruptive advertising experience to mobile device users.

Location-based marketing

Rapid growth of gps-enabled connected mobile devices gave rise to a new category of location-based marketing technologies. Precise user location, typically supplied by a smartphone, can be put to use in ad targeting, in-store marketing, analytics, user profiling and other applications. Location data is usually obtained either from ad impressions, or from apps with access to location services on a user's device.

From the programmatic advertising perspective, the most interesting and common use of location data is ad targeting[xxi]. Precise latitude and longitude information can be supplied directly in the bid request, so advertisers can choose to target only mobile devices in a very specific geographic location. Bid requests coming from interesting locations tend to be more valuable to advertisers, who are willing to pay more. This is unfortunately tempting to fraudsters, who often supply incorrect location data. Also, some apps can update their location less frequently, making it inaccurate. Caution when using mobile location data is advised, and vendors are already offering solutions to address location fraud.

Retailers with physical stores are also finding location data very useful. In addition to lat/long coordinates supplied through gps-enabled smartphones, many retailers are experimenting with indoor location technologies. Beacons based on low-energy Bluetooth (BLE) can accurately track users in-store, often via a branded app on their phones. This data can be used for in-store marketing, including personalized offers, promotions, and reminders that drive conversions and engagement. Retailers can also use location and in-store transaction data in attribution modeling to understand path to purchase and capture offline conversions.

A very interesting, albeit controversial, potential application of location data is behavioral profiling. A lot of insights can be derived from users' movements – the place of residence/work, interests, habits and even purchase intent. Location could be used as a real-world cookie, tracking both behavior as well as the exposure to out-of-home and other advertising. Additionally, location data can be used for profile linking (for example a TV or desktop computer profile in the place of residence with a mobile device). Naturally, using location data for behavioral profiling can easily violate user privacy. Such practices need to be highly regulated.

Cross-device

Cross-device (or cross platform/environment) integration involves the identification of users across their devices/browsers, and the subsequent use of a unified profile (and related data) – for example to make marketing more efficient or perhaps to personalize content. A current challenge is the integration between users' different browsers and mobile devices, but other platforms are coming – including TVs, wearables, or the coming internet of things.

Cookies are not very useful when it comes to cross-device integration, since they either don't exist, or are difficult to utilize beyond desktop. There are two main approaches to identifying users across devices – deterministic and probabilistic. The deterministic approach takes advantage of a unique ID (typically login or e-mail address), guaranteeing reliable user identification regardless of device. On the other hand, the probabilistic method consists in analyzing vast quantities of data (such as device type, browser, operating system, IP address etc.) to merge user profiles based on statistical probability.

Deterministic method is far more precise, but is beyond reach of most companies (apart from giants such as Facebook, Google, Apple or Amazon). This is because most businesses don't require a login to use their services (for example most online news publishers), and consequently only have unique IDs for a small portion of their users. New initiatives aim to overcome this problem, such as publisher co-ops created for the purpose of sharing deterministic IDs. The question with such projects is typically scale, accompanied by privacy and data protection concerns.

So what is cross-device integration good for? In a nutshell, it enables marketers to track the entire consumer journey as it unfolds across all digital touch points – regardless of whether they happen on desktop, mobile, or any other device. It is a prerequisite for proper one-to-one marketing, from basic targeting to an individualized campaign management. This can involve for example global campaign frequency capping, or sequential messaging. With cross-device integration, marketers can measure campaigns across multiple screens and attribute results correctly at the end.

Another use case for cross-device integration is data consolidation. Previously isolated user profiles related to the same user can be merged, creating a richer, more accurate picture of reality. This increases data quality, applicability and value.

Cross-device integration shows a great promise, and is a game-changer for the ad tech industry. However, there are some concerns around the future market development and the potential power some big players might gain. At the same time, user privacy rights around tracking need to be considered and respected, offering a choice to easily opt out.

6 CURRENT ISSUES

Just like any emerging technology, programmatic advertising currently faces several challenges widely discussed within digital ad industry. This chapter will provide a brief introduction to some of them – including issues of fraud, viewability, ad blocking, attribution, and privacy.

Fraud

In the digital advertising world, fraud is a broad term encompassing wide range of unethical (or outright illegal) activities, designed to stealthily divert some of the advertising spend into the pockets of its perpetrators. Fraudsters attempt to game the advertising ecosystem by artificially inflating metrics such as impressions, clicks or conversions, while masquerading as organic activity. They appear to create value for advertisers, but in fact deliver no real impact.

Probably the most common type of fraud is nonhuman traffic (NHT), where deceptive computer programs (bots) mimic desired behavior of real users on the web. Bots are used to register impressions, clicks or influence other metrics, pretending they are actual humans. More sophisticated bots can fake conversions (for example fill out a lead-generation form) or let themselves be retargeted. This type of fraud is so prevalent, that the term "fraud" is often used interchangeably with NHT. Exact scale of nonhuman traffic is not known, as it varies greatly by region, publisher, or exchange.

Bots often run on internet user's computers, in the form of malware operating in the background without anyone noticing. It is increasingly common to use data centers to run bot networks though, as these are easier to manage and can be deployed on a much larger scale. Nonhuman traffic can be readily bought (often by less scrupulous or unwitting publishers), or is pushed into the advertising ecosystem through ad networks and exchanges.

There are other types of fraud besides nonhuman traffic. Ads can be for example served stacked on top of each other, or in tiny 1x1 pixel frames. Publisher domain might also be manipulated, to make inventory appear more valuable – so called domain laundering. Another fraudulent technique is cookie stuffing, where fraudsters drop illegitimate cookies in order to fool affiliate programs and get compensation for contributing to a sale. Fraudsters also set up networks of fake sites, built only for advertising with no valuable content (and usually with very little human traffic).

As mobile ad spend increases, fraud is gradually expanding into this new territory. Some fraud types are the same (such as NHT), but new ones have appeared that are specific to mobile. A lot of fraud is related to the app ecosystem, particularly when it comes to driving app downloads and in-app purchases. For example, it is easy to fake app installs if they are measured only by click metrics. Advertisers need to analyze subsequent app usage and compare it to how real users have behaved in the past, in order to determine if the installs are legitimate.

In-app purchases are subject to fraud as well, as many of them are never actually paid for (but fraudsters get credited and paid as if real purchases happened). Another type of fraud specific to mobile is manipulation of location data. As noted previously, impressions with interesting location data tend to be more valuable to advertisers, making it attractive for fraudsters to add fake coordinates to a bid request. These are naturally just some of the scams within the ad ecosystem, and new ways of deceiving honest players are being developed every day. This makes it very difficult to manage, let alone eradicate fraudulent activities.

As part of an industry-wide effort to tackle fraud, IAB formed the Trustworthy Accountability Group (TAG)[xxii], which was already introduced in chapter two. While TAG and other organizations offer insights and direction on how to tackle fraud, responsibility for eradicating it lies with every honest participant in the digital advertising ecosystem – particularly publishers and advertisers.

Publishers differ in their stance towards fraud. To most legitimate and premium publishers, fraud is a serious issue as it devalues honest impressions seen by real humans. If fraud was eradicated, these publishers would profit substantially. On the other hand, there are publishers who thrive on fraud. Their business models are often based on arbitrage – buying cheap, mostly nonhuman traffic, and turning it into more expensive impressions sold to advertisers. Such arbitrage models would not work with real human traffic, as it is too expensive to purchase.

Many publishers are also caught in-between, permitting some level of fraud on their properties either knowingly, or without being aware of it. Publishers might choose to buy some traffic to increase their available inventory or make it cheaper, due to competitive and market pressures. Traffic is also sometimes bought when publishers embark on new projects, to quickly build marketable audiences for them. It is possible to buy mostly human traffic, and content discovery companies such as Taboola or Outbrain specialize in providing it. Publishers can decide to go this route, but it tends to be too expensive for arbitrage and unsustainable in the long run to rely solely on purchased human traffic. They can also buy very cheap traffic, but it is likely to be nonhuman. All in all, publishers have a lot of control over fraud, which is why the level of NHT fraud varies greatly among them.

Advertisers stand to lose the most to ad fraud, as their budgets could be diverted from campaigns and deliver no impact in return. One way to combat ad fraud is to look beyond simple metrics when analyzing campaigns (impressions or CTR for example), as these are easy to manipulate artificially. Instead, advertisers should focus more on the end goal metrics, such as return on investment or real conversions. As fraudulent activities have net negative ROI, advertisers who optimize towards the right metrics should be able to eliminate most of them from their campaigns. Of course, it is hard to use such metrics for evaluating branding campaigns. Here, advertisers can get help from a number of vendors specializing in ad fraud identification and filtering (often alongside viewability measurement). Some of the well-known players offering anti-fraud solutions include DoubleVerify, Integral Ad Science, Forensiq or White Ops.

Fraud is often discussed together with viewability, albeit they are fundamentally different issues. With fraud, the question is typically whether an ad was served to a human. Viewability then determines if that human had an opportunity to see the ad. However, both issues are related to advertising efficiency. If advertisers spend part of their budgets on ads which are served to bots, or which could never have been seen by human users, their return on investment decreases. It has to be noted though, that solving ad fraud comes before solving viewability – if an impression gets served to a bot, it doesn't matter anymore whether it was viewable or not.

Viewability

Ad viewability is broadly defined as the opportunity for an ad to be seen. It has become an important issue, as many advertisers realized that a large proportion of impressions they pay for not only goes unseen, but could never have been seen by human users in the first place. This is due to a number of reasons, some more legitimate than others. For example, user might scroll through a page too quickly to have a chance to see an ad. Or the ads might be served on a page section that never comes into view of the user (below the fold for example). Many impressions are also served fraudulently, in particular to non-human traffic.

The Media Rating Council (MRC) classifies an ad impression as viewable, if at least 50 % of the ad pixels were contained in the viewable space of the browser window, on an in-focus browser tab, for at least one continuous second post ad render. For larger formats, 30 % of the ad pixels are sufficient to qualify within this definition. Video ad impressions require 50 % of the pixels for two seconds to be considered viewable. Requirements are the same for mobile viewability (50 % of pixels for one second for display, two seconds for video), both on mobile web and within apps.

Ad viewability rates vary across publishers, (usually in the range of 50-70 %), depending on inventory quality and viewability measurement vendor. Although some advertisers would like to see 100 % viewability for their campaigns, the currently accepted standard is 70 % (but is entirely up to the parties involved), due to technological and commercial limitations. IAB considers the 70 % standard only temporary, with a view of increasing it in the future.

A number of vendors offer viewability measurement, each using a slightly different methodology. While there is a standard on what constitutes a viewable impression, there is no exact standard of measuring it. Two methodologies are commonly used for viewability measurement – geometric, and browser optimization. With the geometric method, ad position is considered relative to the browser window on a page to determine whether an ad is viewable. This method is reliable, but can't be used when ads are served in iframes. Alternatively, browser optimization takes advantage of the fact that browsers know what is in view and what is not, and manage resources accordingly. Browser optimization can be used with iframes, but often makes measurement inconsistent between vendors. Exact implementation and combination of the two methodologies varies by vendor and their sophistication.

Major vendors are accredited by the MRC, and many offer measurement options beyond the minimum viewability standard. Some of the well-known players in this space include DoubleVerify, Integral Ad Science, comScore, Moat, AppNexus, Chartbeat, RealVu, Google ActiveView, OnScroll, Sizmek and others. To many advertisers and publishers alike, it is important that viewability is measured independently, and the figures can be relied on. Unfortunately, due to different vendor methodologies, viewability rates are still inconsistent and subject to much debate.

One of the biggest reasons why viewability rates differ among vendors is fraud detection and handling. When detected, non-human traffic impressions should be classified as non-viewable. While some vendors are very good at recognizing fraud and classifying impressions accordingly, others are not as sophisticated or make very little effort. The better a vendor is at detecting fraud, the lower their viewability rates might become. Differences can be also due to use of sampling by some vendors as opposed to measuring every impression. Other factors include different measurability rate (percentage of impressions that the vendor is able to measure), measuring the actual ad instead of the ad slot, and random factors such as code loading times.

Viewability is a hot topic not only for advertisers, but also for publishers. They need to know what the viewability rate of their inventory is with different providers, in order to guarantee viewability thresholds to advertisers. Given the differences in reported viewability among vendors, publishers are in a difficult situation. If an advertiser is using a different viewability vendor than a publisher, there is a high chance of discrepancy and potential under-delivery. It might be safer to over-deliver, but this represents inefficiency on the publisher side. Inventory forecasting in this situation can become a nightmare. As viewable impressions gradually become the industry standard, publishers also need to work on optimizing their inventory for viewability to limit impact on their bottom lines.

As beneficial as viewability measurement undoubtedly is, it poses some challenges when it comes to programmatic advertising. Direct campaigns usually have higher viewability than inventory bought programmatically, since a lot of the inventory offered programmatically is remnant and non-premium. This varies greatly by region and publisher though. Advertisers need to understand that executing a large-scale campaign with a high viewability requirement can be difficult to do programmatically. Viewability in various placements can be estimated, but is never guaranteed until the ad is served and classified as viewable. A common solution to this problem is to only bid for impressions with high probability of being viewable (based on historical figures for example), but it might not be possible to achieve sufficient scale with this approach.

With all the buzz surrounding viewability, it is good to keep in mind that a viewable ad was not necessarily seen, let alone engaged with. Viewability by itself doesn't guarantee impact, and too much emphasis on this single metric might even be counterproductive. To illustrate, one way to increase campaign viewability rate is to use smaller ad formats, which tend to have a higher chance of meeting the MRC viewability standard compared to large formats. Smaller formats, albeit viewable, are often ignored by users though – generating no impact at all. Viewability therefore needs to be considered in the context of engagement and results, not just as a standalone metric.

Given the large number of viewability vendors with inconsistent methodologies, and the resulting industry problems, viewability measurement consolidation seems inevitable. This will go hand in hand with solving other issues, in particular fraud or attribution analysis. Measurement of viewability is also likely to grow far beyond the current standard, and merge with broader user engagement and impact measurement across digital media. This is especially true for video, where the minimum viewability standard doesn't reflect its creative and impact potential.

Ad blocking

Ad blocking is an increasingly common practice of using a program to remove advertising while browsing the internet or using apps. The ad blocking trend has accelerated since 2013, and poses a threat to the current business models of many publishers and app developers. While exact numbers vary, it is clear that ad blocking is prevalent among younger demographics (particularly young males), and in some regions – including Germany and central/eastern Europe.

Reasons for ad blocking popularity are pretty straightforward. Many users find that there are too many low quality or annoying ads on their favorite websites, and are tired of always having to look for the elusive x to close an ad. The widespread practice of retargeting is partly to blame as well, increasing privacy concerns. Ads (particularly rich media and some novel formats) can have negative impact on page load times – this is even worse on mobile, where the connection speed and data plans are still a significant limitation. Last but not least, ad blockers have recently become much easier to install – Apple has for instance allowed content blocking on iOS.

Ad blocking is a major problem for many publishers and app developers, who depend on advertising as their main source of revenue. For years, there used to be a clear (albeit often not understood) value exchange between publishers and consumers – free content for exposure to advertising. Ad blocking breaks this value exchange, as publishers no longer get anything back for the content that often costs a lot to produce. Some of the value just disappears, while ad blocking companies try to capture the rest by having publishers and advertisers pay for whitelisting their ads. This practice is highly controversial and subject to legal disputes. The strongest weapon publishers have to fight ad blocking is control of their content, but the implementation might be tricky.

The impact of ad blocking on publishers and the entire advertising ecosystem is still hard to predict. New business models will need to be explored, such as subscriptions, cross-domain paywalls, paid downloads, or shift to native advertising. The popularity of ad blocking shows that consumers are not happy with the status quo, but there are big risks to content production, availability and control in the future as well. As for programmatic advertising, ad blocking might decrease ad inventory in the open ecosystem, and make some target segments harder to reach.

Attribution

It is helpful to view attribution as a tool for optimizing the marketing spend to maximize return on investment. In an ideal world, marketers would know exactly how each part of their communication mix contributes to a desired outcome (usually conversions), and attribute credit accordingly. Activities, which deliver the highest incremental return on investment, would then receive a bigger portion of the marketing budget – while those that don't contribute would be cut from the plan. Eventually, budget should be allocated in an optimal way for maximum ROI. In reality, attribution is not nearly this straightforward, and can be tricky (if not impossible) to implement in a true and useful way.

Most attribution solutions available and widely used today only enable attribution across the digital media channels (such as social, search, display, affiliate etc.) on a single screen. Doing attribution across multiple screens is a whole new ballgame, while correctly attributing across online and offline is reserved only for the most sophisticated advertisers[xxiii].

Naturally, potential customers normally encounter several "screens" in the course of a marketing campaign, from desktop and mobile through TV to channels like radio or outdoor advertising. Less tangible factors, such as brand awareness, come into play as well. And when potential customers finally convert, it often happens offline. It is therefore very important for marketers to understand exactly which campaign touch points (such as views or clicks) and outcomes are captured by their attribution solution, and use the tool appropriately.

Let's now briefly discuss the elephant in the room – last-touch attribution. This is possibly the most common attribution model, where the entire credit for a conversion goes to the last campaign touch point (either last-click or last-view) before it happened. Apart from the fact that it usually captures only part of reality (some digital channels on a single screen, and often only online conversions), last-touch attribution can greatly under-value some channels and is prone to being gamed.

If all credit goes to the very last touch point, channels which target potential customers who are close to con-version (such as paid search or retargeting) have an up-per hand. Many of these conversions would have hap-pened anyway, but the channels are credited nonethe-less. On the other hand, channels higher up the market-ing funnel, which could bring new customers and incre-mental conversions (typically prospecting activities), of-ten get no credit at all.

The last-touch attribution model can be easily gamed as well. A glaring example of this is excessive retarget-ing, optimized to capture the last-touch just before a conversion. To an unwitting marketer, it would seem like retargeting is bringing lots of cheap conversions, while other channels pale in comparison. In reality, re-targeting is just usurping all the credit, thanks to last-touch attribution model. Another form of gaming last-touch attribution is purchasing lots of very cheap inven-tory (often not even viewable), with hope of encounter-ing a user as the last touch point before a conversion. Alternatively, inventory can be purchased selectively on sites where potential customers are highly likely to go just before a conversion, such as coupon or review sites.

Despite all of its shortcomings, last-touch attribution remains widely used across digital ad industry, and is often the default option in analytics platforms. Other common attribution models include first-touch, even, time decay or positional. The first-touch model gives all the credit to the first channel encountered on a path to conversion. The even model gives credit to all channels evenly, while time decay gives more credit to channels encountered closer to conversion. The positional model gives different credit to first, last and middle channels on the path. Some of these models are useless, but not all – while first touch should be avoided, others are potentially more fair and harder to game than last-touch attribution.

More sophisticated advertisers can also create bespoke attribution models, and improve on them over time. These models can be either static, with pre-defined weights for credit distribution, or dynamic, where machine-learning and advanced algorithms distribute credit according to merit.

Validating and improving attribution models is difficult, and involves a lot of testing and experimentation. For example, it is not easy to distinguish between mere correlation and actual causation between a marketing campaign across various channels and conversions.

Some of the conversions would have happened anyway, and the channels involved in a campaign should get no credit for them if the aim is to optimize for maximum ROI. An attribution model should only reward incremental conversions, but these are not easy to separate. Testing against control groups or establishing a baseline number of conversions are some of the options to explore.

Further enhancements of attribution models could involve separate approaches for retargeting and prospecting campaigns, in order to protect credit that should go to prospecting. Advertisers with large budgets can also bring more channels and conversions into the model – particularly through cross-device matching and attribution of offline conversions. Including even all digital channels is difficult though, as various advertising systems often don't accept external pixel tracking.

To conclude this section, attribution is a fantastic tool for optimizing the marketing spend to maximize ROI. However, there is still a long way to go before the tool is perfect, so it is critical to understand its limitations and interpret any resulting data accordingly. Given its prevalence and obvious flaws, advertisers should be particularly wary of the last-touch attribution model. Even if not perfect, a sensible attribution model can still provide a lot of value despite its limitations. For many advertisers, it might not be worth investing into more advanced solutions at the moment. A lot of progress can be expected in this area in the near future, so better and cheaper attribution methods should be available soon.

Privacy

Online privacy is a very complex topic, involving intricate technical, legal and ethical aspects. At the heart is the possibility to collect personal data on an unprecedented scale, enabled by rapid digitalization of many aspects of human existence. Common activities like internet browsing, social media and web application use, online communication as well as wearing of smart devices can all leave a digital trace. This data can be collected, stored and analyzed, and is often used for marketing or security purposes.

Personal data ownership (anonymous or not) is a precious asset, especially if the information is unique, valuable and on a large scale. Most of this data is owned or controlled by relatively few private companies, and can be potentially accessed by government agencies as well. A privacy controversy arises from the fact that the general public has a limited knowledge of this practice, and little control over their personal data.

From the user perspective, some level of privacy has been lost or given up, often without conscious consent. Many online services require users to grant data ownership generated by using the service to service provider, in exchange for free access. This trade-off can be justified by subsequent data utilization to make the service better, or monetization helping to fund the service. However, users frequently agree to terms of use without reading or thoroughly understanding them, and are unaware of the value exchange they are making. The extent to which users are consciously willing to trade their personal data for free services therefore remains questionable.

From the marketer perspective, user data can significantly improve the efficiency and the quality of customer relationships. Data ownership or access constitutes an unquestionable competitive advantage, enabling a whole new level of communication targeting and relationship management. But marketers need to be careful – privacy concerns can lead to erosion of trust, with potentially grave consequences.

Given the importance and sensitivity of maintaining privacy in the digital world, government laws and industry self-regulation initiatives strive to keep up with technology and establish rules and best practices for handling user information. Regulation is not uniform around the world, and for the most part applies on a national or regional basis.

Examples of government regulation in the USA include Electronic Communications Privacy Act (ECPA), Children's Online Privacy Protection Act (COPPA), or Children's Internet Protection Act (CIPA). In the EU, privacy is regulated by directives such as ePrivacy Directive or Data Protection Directive, soon to be superseded by the General Data Protection Regulation (GDPR). Individual countries have their own laws and regulations as well, with Germany being a vocal proponent of strict privacy protection.

In addition to external regulation, the industry is working on simultaneous self-regulation. There's a Self-Regulatory Program for Online Behavioral Advertising backed by the Digital Advertising Alliance (DAA), in cooperation with the Interactive Advertising Bureau (IAB), Association of National Advertisers (ANA), American Association of Advertising Agencies (4A's) the Direct Marketing Association (DMA) and the Council of Better Business Bureaus (CBBB)[xxiv]. A notable feature of this program is an advertising option icon to be displayed alongside online ads, giving access to data collection disclosure statement together with an opt-out option.

Under all the various laws and regulations, not all user data is protected equally. There's a special class of sensitive data that receives a higher level of protection – Personally Identifiable Information (PII). PII includes any data that can either alone, or in combination with other data, identify an individual person. Data such as name, address, social security/passport/national ID number, credit card numbers, phone number or date of birth typically fall under PII. Depending on applicable legislation, such data can often be collected and stored only by registered or designated organizations, and must be well protected. Only non-PII data should be used for behavioral targeting.

As legislators and the general public become more aware of potential privacy risks in the digital era, tighter regulation can be expected. Individuals will likely be given more control over the collection and use of their personal data, along with clearer information about the benefits and possible threats. Some categories of highly sensitive data (such as information about specific health conditions) will probably be put strictly off-limits, or at least under government scrutiny. Clear rules on who, how, and when can collect what data are needed, in adherence to public interest.

Regardless of the future shape of privacy regulation, it is clear that a major shift is under way. It remains up to the digital marketing industry to act ethically where laws are absent or unclear, and to do its part in protecting internet users and maintaining their trust.

7 NEW FORMATS AND CHANNELS

Programmatic advertising, as is often the case with disruptive technologies, started out by automating sales of low-end, remnant inventory. Over time, programmatic moved up to encompass pretty much every kind of digital inventory – all the way to the most premium. New, engaging and highly visual formats – like rich media, video or native – are increasingly available through programmatic channels. Additionally, advertising channels are gradually becoming automated, from TV to audio, out-of-home and print.

With the advent of more premium inventory and exciting new channels, digital branding campaigns can now be executed programmatically, often through a single platform. This is great news for big brand advertisers, who are increasingly shifting their budgets from traditional direct buys to automated channels. In this chapter, we will look at some of the new formats and channels, which are quickly becoming available programmatically.

Rich media

Rich media formats have been around for a while, but only recently are becoming widely available through programmatic channels. In a nutshell, rich media offer more engagement, interaction and impact compared to static banner ads, and come in many guises. They can contain more advanced (and bandwidth heavy) features, such as video or audio. Depending on the specific rich media format, an ad might cover the page, expand, push content aside, or allow user scrolling through a multi-part creative.

The promise and appeal of programmatic rich media is in the combination of the high engagement of interactive rich media formats, with precise targeting available programmatically. Taking advantage of both, brands can now hope to deliver very impactful campaigns with minimal waste of valuable budgets.

To enable reliable rich media ad delivery, HTML5 is rapidly becoming the new standard for ad creative. The latest version of HTML is able to efficiently handle content such as embedded video or audio, as well as very complex interactive creatives. Possibilities offered by HTML5, coupled with unavailability of Adobe Flash on many devices, makes this standard a natural choice for programmatic rich media.

Of course, implementing and testing rich media formats is much more complex and difficult on the publisher side, compared to standard banner ads. Rich media-ready inventory availability thus varies by publisher, and only some formats might be offered. To speed up adoption of rich media, the IAB is constantly developing common standards for individual formats, so that publishers and advertisers can work towards the same specifications. Rich media format details can be found on the IAB website[xxv], along with "Rising Stars" formats – both are commonly grouped together and referred to simply as rich media.

IAB rich media formats include in-banner video, interstitials, expandables, and floating ads. With the in-banner video, a video ad is delivered within a standard ad placement, instead of a dedicated video player. Interstitial ads appear either full screen, or as an overlay between pages as a user is browsing a website. Expandable ads can be enlarged beyond the initial dimensions of their original placement. Expansion happens automatically, or following user interaction. Finally, floating ads appear on top of page content.

IAB rising stars formats are for example filmstrip, billboard, pushdown or sidekick. With a filmstrip, an ad is divided into five 300x600 pixel segments a user can scroll through. A billboard ad is designed to be displayed prominently inline with a publisher's content, with options for rich interactivity. Pushdown ad is an expanding format, which (unlike most expandable ads) pushes down the page content. A sidekick, upon user interaction, pushes the page content to the left to display a canvas of up to 970x550 pixels.

Naturally, rich media and rising stars formats exist on mobile as well. Examples of mobile rich media include smartphone rich interstitial, or smartphone rich expandable banner. Some of the mobile rising stars are adhesion banner, slider, or filmstrip.

Programmatic video ads

Programmatic video ads are quickly becoming a standard part of digital campaigns, and for many good reasons. It is difficult to challenge video as the ultimate engagement and brand-building format. With precise targeting data available in the programmatic ecosystem, high-impact video ads can be delivered to a very responsive audience. If executed well, a programmatic video campaign can easily become the best performing part of digital media plan. Although there is still some way to go with programmatic TV, video inventory availability is rapidly growing – particularly on desktop and mobile.

Standardization was critical for programmatic video growth. Without it, the digital video inventory would remain fragmented across publishers using different standards, and advertisers wouldn't be able to reach the desired scale and efficiency of their campaigns. The IAB has been developing video standards, commonly known as IAB Video Suite[xxvi]. This suite comprises three standalone protocols, which are designed to work together, while offering implementation flexibility at the same time – VAST, VPAID and VMAP.

Video Ad-Serving Template (VAST) is a protocol for serving in-stream video ads, which enables compliant video players to accept a common ad response format, and therefore any VAST-compliant video ad. The Video Player-Ad Interface Definition (VPAID) is a communication protocol which facilitates ad interaction and event reporting. Finally, the Video Multiple Ad Playlist (VMAP) protocol enables video content owners to define ad break placement, even if they don't have control of the video player or content distribution network.

As far as programmatic video advertising formats go, they fall into two categories – in-stream and out-stream. In-stream ads appear within a dedicated video player, as part of viewed content stream. The most common format is pre-roll, appearing at the very beginning before video content itself. Pre-roll ad can be usually skipped after a few seconds. Mid-roll ads appear somewhere between the beginning and the end of video content. There can be multiple mid-roll ads, which usually have higher completion rates compared to pre- and post-rolls. Post-roll ads are placed at the end, once the video content finishes.

Out-stream video ads don't require a dedicated video player, let alone a piece of video content to appear against. Individual vendors offer different out-stream formats, but a pretty common one is in-text video ad. Here, video ad appears as user scrolls down while reading page content. Content parts to accommodate a video ad, which disappears once the ad is finished. Out-stream ads offer a convenient solution to the lack of premium video inventory, and a new revenue stream for publishers.

A special category of programmatic video inventory is in-banner video. Here, video ad is served within a standard banner placement. In-banner video is easy to implement and run, but offers very limited user engagement and overall impact. Furthermore, it can lead to bad user experience, due to the common auto play use and resulting slow page loading. Despite the drawbacks, low price and wide supply make this video ad format very common.

Similar to other programmatic formats, digital video ads can be sold on a CPM (cost per thousand) basis. However, other metrics can be used as well, such as CPCV (cost per completed view) or CPE (cost per engagement). Some metrics can take it a step further, taking into account ad viewability for example.

With unparalleled user engagement potential and expanding inventory supply, programmatic video is set for dynamic growth in the near future. Mobile programmatic video is the next frontier, and new standards and formats can be expected.

Programmatic native

Native advertising is currently one of the hottest trends in programmatic. Native ads are designed to blend into the surrounding content by mimicking its format and functionality. They strive not to feel like advertising, to which many internet users have become blind or resentful. A promise of less interruptive ad experience is indeed an alluring one, particularly if coupled with the scale and efficiency of programmatic technology. With the success of social native on Facebook or Twitter, open programmatic ecosystem is getting ready to introduce native to the rest of the web.

There are six broad native formats identified by the IAB – in-feed units, paid search units, recommendation widgets, promoted listings, in-ad with native element units, and custom units[xxvii]. The in-feed ad units appear among other content in the main feed, and are often prepared in cooperation with the individual publishers. IAB offers a detailed overview of the in-feed format, paying special attention to nuances of placing native ads in content, social and product feeds[xxviii]. Paid search native units present their content in a layout and format very similar to organic search results, but must be properly disclosed. With recommendation widgets, a "widget" is responsible for delivering an ad or content link. These ads, while still classified as native, usually don't match the design or function of surrounding content. Promoted listings, just like native paid search ads, look very similar to surrounding "organic" product listings, but again must be properly disclosed. In-ad native units fit within standard IAB ad units, but contain native elements. All other native formats fall into custom native.

Given the large variety of native ad formats, standards are critical for large-scale automation. Led by the Native Advertising Task Force, IAB has been working on a specification that would enable programmatic trading in native ads. The first iteration of this specification, called OpenRTB Native Ads API Specification[xxix], was released as part of OpenRTB protocol (version 2.3[xxx]). Native ads are handled as a collection of assets (such as ad title, logo, icon, video, descriptive text, price, etc.), delivered and assembled for each impression according to the bid request specification.

The OpenRTB native sub-protocol offers publishers the flexibility to adjust the look and feel of native ads which are to be displayed on their inventory, while enabling scalability for advertisers. However, it is much more technologically demanding to build a native ad from creative assets on the fly, so publishers need access to a native-ready SSP. On the buy side, many DSPs are ready for programmatic native, and are able to trade such impressions. In terms of technology, native ads can already be traded programmatically, and are expected to grow in market share as more publishers and advertisers get on board.

Despite all the optimism, there's an inherent controversy to native ads. They work so well because they don't look like ads – which can easily make them misleading to consumers as to their commercial intent. It is therefore critical that native ads are very clearly disclosed, if there is any risk that they could be taken for editorial content. For instance, Federal Trade Commission in the US is very strict when it comes to native advertising disclosure. In its Native Advertising guide, the FTC strives to protect consumers from misleading and deceptive advertising by setting very clear and detailed rules for ad appearance and disclosure[xxxi]. Companies that don't comply with FTC guidelines are under threat of legal action. Advertisers have the primary responsibility here, but other parties could be judged responsible as well.

Native advertising shows high promise, with potential of alleviating some of the ills associated with standard advertising. With the introduction of an open programmatic native standard and development of the necessary trading technology, it can be expected that this format will rapidly grow beyond social. However, there is a thin line between native used right, and consumer deception. All players in the ecosystem, advertisers in particular, need to use native responsibly if it is to fulfill its promise if making digital advertising better.

Programmatic TV

TV is an exciting new frontier for advertising automation, given its prominence as the ultimate advertising medium. There's no better way of building brands at scale, than through high-quality visual and audio experiences on a large screen. TV advertising still commands a lion's share of marketing budgets, but is starting to lag behind digital advertising in terms of technology and campaign execution. Disruption of status quo is under way, and is widely expected to come in the form of programmatic TV.

Two aspects are critical when we talk about programmatic TV – automation and audience data. The goal is to be able to execute an automated campaign targeted at a distinct and precise audience across multiple screens, including television.

Which channels comprise "television" depends on each particular market – from traditional linear TV (TV with scheduled program) to increasingly popular video-on-demand and streaming services. To the consumers and marketers alike, distinction between these channels is quickly disappearing. However, digital video channels have an upper hand in terms of readiness for TV's programmatic future.

When it comes to automation, digital video inventory is much easier to prepare for programmatic trading. The big challenge is linear TV, where progress has been fairly slow so far. Thanks to high demand and limited supply of premium inventory, particularly when it comes to primetime shows, automation doesn't promise much short-term financial gain. Long-tail inventory (local or niche shows for example) is likely to be automated first, as this can help increase its value to potential buyers. The process of automating linear TV will be gradual, driven by advertiser pressure and challenge from digital video channels.

Unlike some digital channels where programmatic is already thriving, television, especially linear, doesn't yet offer much individual (or household) audience data. Limited offline and digital data is used during TV campaign planning and execution, but this is often a manual process. Such data might include credit/credit card data, car registration data, or set-top box data (commonly referred to as addressable TV). For digital video though, the situation is very different. Behavioral and other targeting data can be integrated in an automated way, particularly if a login and a registration is required to use a service. As many big brands start accumulating their own customer data and building strategies around it, they will push to use it on TV screens as well.

Programmatic TV, encompassing automation and audience data usage, will bring a number of benefits. The possibility to target TV advertising to a very granular audience segment will increase campaign efficiency of many advertisers, and attract new ones for whom television reach used to be too broad. The automation of previously manual processes will drive costs down both for inventory buyers, as well as sellers. Sellers are also likely to benefit from better yield management platforms, reporting, and increased value of some non-premium inventory (niche or local shows for example). For advertisers and their agencies, programmatic TV will offer previously unthinkable flexibility in campaign management, with performance metrics available while ads are still running.

Probably the greatest potential benefit of programmatic TV is enablement of true cross-screen (television, desktop, mobile, possibly other channels) campaign planning, delivery and measurement. Once television advertising is automated and data-driven, there is no reason it couldn't be managed within the same platform along with other advertising media and channels. This would be a huge step forward when it comes to attribution and subsequent marketing spend optimization. Universal advertising platforms of this kind will have a lot of appeal, but it remains to be seen if they emerge as open or closed ecosystems.

Some of the greatest barriers on the road to programmatic TV lie in a long history of television as a prominent and independent advertising channel. There's little short-term financial incentive to move away from direct sales, exacerbated by fear of inventory commoditization. Legacy infrastructure makes it difficult to implement automation and integrate data, but digital video providers are side-stepping this issue. There might also be legal barriers in some markets, with often cumbersome ad approval process. Finally, given the complexity of programmatic technologies, lack of skilled staff to implement changes can become a real challenge.

It will take some time before programmatic TV arrives at a critical scale. There is no doubt though that potential benefits are massive, and any hurdles can be gradually overcome. Marketers and TV executives should become comfortable with and ready for the future, as automated, data-enabled, and integrated television advertising at scale will be the ultimate manifestation of what programmatic can deliver.

Programmatic print

Print publishers are starting to experiment with programmatic trading technologies applied to print ads. Time Inc., a major US magazine publisher, is currently at the forefront of this trend[xxxii]. Partnering with Media-Math (a demand-side platform), Time Inc. allows advertisers to purchase print ads in a similar fashion to digital advertising. There is even an option to target specific audiences (based on magazine reader surveys).

While using programmatic ecosystem to trade print ads could simplify the buying process and attract new demand for publishers, some major issues when compared to digital remain. These include for instance high operational and logistical costs of personalizing print beyond very broad audience segments, or impact measurement.

Programmatic audio

With the rapid growth of digital audio – from music streaming services, podcasts, digital radio to music social networks – there's a ripe opportunity to make audio ad trading programmatic. To facilitate this transition, the IAB released Digital Audio Ad Serving Template (DAAST) – a set of specifications for audio ad delivery, execution and reporting across many devices and platforms[xxxiii]. A number of audio ad exchanges already exist, including Triton with the a2x audio ad exchange[xxxiv] in the United States and elsewhere, or the Digital Advertising Exchange (DAX) under Global radio[xxxv] in the UK.

A huge advantage of audio ads, compared to display, is the potentially undivided attention of listeners. While a display ad might appear on a page along with several other ads and content itself, audio ads are exclusive within an audio stream. Just like display ads, programmatic audio can support the use of data for audience targeting. Unlike print however, costs and complexity of personalization can remain relatively low.

Although audio ad personalization is possible in terms of technology, consumer privacy concerns and potential alienation are open issues. Measurement and attribution is a bit tricky as well – commonly used listen-through rate metric doesn't necessarily capture active user attention. With the growing advertiser demand, it is likely that solutions for the remaining hurdles will be found, and programmatic audio will quickly follow in the footsteps of programmatic display.

Programmatic out-of-home

Another frontier where programmatic ad trading is gradually making progress is digital out-of-home (DOOH). Digital screens in public places, such as shopping malls, transportation hubs, stadiums, or gyms can be used to reach hundreds of people simultaneously in an automated fashion. Ads can be precisely targeted in terms of location and time, but other data will likely be added – such as current weather or (albeit controversial) facial recognition for one-to-one personalization[xxxvi].

Unlike programmatic display, where each impression is traded individually, DOOH impressions are traded in bundles based on a screen's current audience size estimate on a CPM basis. Digital out-of-home is closely linked to location data collected from devices like smartphones or in-store beacons. With a complete user location and purchase data profile, DOOH can be easily plugged into attribution models. Despite programmatic out-of-home being currently limited to digital screens, it can be expected to grow – if it proves its value.

ABOUT THE AUTHOR

Dominik Kosorin works for the Czech Publisher Exchange, helping to grow programmatic advertising in the Czech Republic and beyond. He lives in Prague with a wonderful wife and an amazing son.

Twitter: @dkosorin

LinkedIn: www.linkedin.com/in/dominikkosorin

E-mail: introduction.to.programmatic@gmail.com

REFERENCES

[i] Fraser, Jeff. " Publicis ditches the agency trading desk." Marketing, February 17, 2015. http://www.marketingmag.ca/advantage/publicis-ditches-the-agency-trading-desk-138032

[ii] Siegel, Emily. "The future of agency trading desks: evolve or die." Digiday.com, March 3, 2015. http://digiday.com/agencies/future-agency-trading-desks-evolve-die

[iii] La Place Media. http://laplacemedia.com

[iv] Reagan, Romany. "Matej Novak, MD, Czech Publisher Exchange Discusses the Premium Publisher Consortium." ExchangeWire.com, September 12, 2013. https://www.exchangewire.com/blog/2013/09/12/matej-novak-md-czech-publisher-exchange-discusses-the-premium-publisher-consortium

[v] The Interactive Advertising Bureau. http://www.iab.com/

[vi] Trustworthy Accountability Group. https://www.tagtoday.net

[vii] Media Rating Council. http://mediaratingcouncil.org

[viii] Federal Trade Commission. https://www.ftc.gov

[ix] The Interactive Advertising Bureau. "Programmatic and automation – the publishers` perspective." Iab.net, 2013. http://www.iab.net/media/file/IAB_Digital_Simplified_Programmatic_Sept_2013.pdf

[x] PwC/The Interactive Advertising Bureau. "IAB Programmatic Revenue Report 2014 Results." Iab.com, July, 2015. http://www.iab.com/wp-content/uploads/2015/07/PwC_IAB_Programmatic_Study.pdf

xi The Interactive Advertising Bureau. http://www.iab.com

xii The Interactive Advertising Bureau. "Programmatic and automation – the pub-lishers` perspective." Iab.net, 2013. http://www.iab.net/me-dia/file/IAB_Digital_Simplified_Programmatic_Sept_2013.pdf

xiii Nahum, Jed. "Header Bidding Killed Programmatic Direct." AdExchanger.com, January 8, 2016. http://adexchanger.com/data-driven-think-ing/header-bidding-killed-programmatic-direct/

xiv Paparo, Ari. "The Strategic Implications Of Header Bidding." AdExchanger.com, October 23, 2015. http://adexchanger.com/the-sell-sider/the-strategic-implications-of-header-bidding/

xvThe Interactive Advertising Bureau. "Understanding mobile cookies." Iab.net, June 11, 2013. http://www.iab.net/media/file/IABDigitalSimplifiedMobileCook-ies.pdf

xvi Apple Support. "Opt out of interest-based ads from iAd." Apple.com, Septem-ber 15, 2015. https://support.apple.com/en-us/HT202074

xvii The Interactive Advertising Bureau. "IAB Mobile Programmatic Playbook." Iab.com, March 16, 2015. https://www.iab.com/wp-content/up-loads/2015/05/MobileProgrammaticPlaybook.pdf

xviii The Interactive Advertising Bureau. "IAB Mobile Programmatic Playbook." Iab.com, March 16, 2015. https://www.iab.com/wp-content/up-loads/2015/05/MobileProgrammaticPlaybook.pdf

xix The Interactive Advertising Bureau. "Mobile Rich-media Ad Interface Defini-tions (MRAID) v.2.0." Iab.com, April 16, 2013. http://www.iab.com/wp-con-tent/uploads/2015/08/IAB_MRAID_v2_FINAL.pdf

xx The Interactive Advertising Bureau. "Mobile Rich-media Ad Interface Defini-tions (MRAID) v.2.0." Iab.com, April 16, 2013. http://www.iab.com/wp-con-tent/uploads/2015/08/IAB_MRAID_v2_FINAL.pdf

xxi The Interactive Advertising Bureau. "Marketing ROI and Location Data." Iab.com, February, 2015. http://www.iab.com/wp-content/up-loads/2015/05/IAB_Marketing_ROI_x26_Location_Data_WhitePaper.pdf

xxii Trustworthy Accountability Group. https://www.tagtoday.net/

xxiii Kaushik, Avinash. "Multi-channel Attribution Modeling: The Good, Bad and Ugly Models." Kaushik.net, August 12, 2013. http://www.kaushik.net/avi-nash/multi-channel-attribution-modeling-good-bad-ugly-models/

xxiv Digital Advertising Alliance. "Digital Advertising Alliance (DAA) Self-Regula-tory Program." AboutAds.info. http://www.aboutads.info/

xxv The Interactive Advertising Bureau. "Interactive Advertising Bureau – Display & mobile advertising creative format guidelines." Iab.com, 2015. http://www.iab.com/wp-content/up-loads/2015/10/IAB_Display_Mobile_Creative_Guidelines_HTML5_2015.pdf

xxvi The Interactive Advertising Bureau. "Digital Video Suite." Iab.com. http://www.iab.com/guidelines/digital-video-suite/

xxvii The Interactive Advertising Bureau. "The native advertising playbook." Iab.net, December 4, 2013. http://www.iab.net/media/file/IABNativeAdvertis-ingPlaybook.pdf

xxviii The Interactive Advertising Bureau. "IAB Deep Dive on In-Feed Ad Units." Iab.com, July, 2015. http://www.iab.com/wp-content/up-loads/2015/07/IAB_Deep_Dive_on_InFeed_Ad_Units.pdf

xxix The Interactive Advertising Bureau. "OpenRTB Dynamic Native Ads API

Specification Version 1." Iab.net, February, 2015. http://www.iab.net/media/file/OpenRTB-Native-Ads-Specification-1_0-Final.pdf

[xxx] The Interactive Advertising Bureau. "OpenRTB API Specification Version 2.3." Iab.net, November, 2014. http://www.iab.net/media/file/OpenRTB-API-Specification-Version-2-3.pdf

[xxxi] Federal Trade Commission. "Native Advertising: A Guide for Businesses." Ftc.gov, December, 2015. https://www.ftc.gov/tips-advice/business-center/guidance/native-advertising-guide-businesses

[xxxii] Sluis, Sarah. "Time Inc. Adds Audience Categories as 'Programmatic Print' Takes Off. AdExchanger.com, July 31, 2015. http://adexchanger.com/publishers/time-inc-adds-audience-categories-as-programmatic-print-takes-off/

[xxxiii] The Interactive Advertising Bureau. "Digital Audio Ad Serving Template." Iab.com. http://www.iab.com/guidelines/digital-audio-ad-serving-template/

[xxxiv] Triton Digital. "a2x Audio Ad Exchange." Tritondigital.com. https://www.tritondigital.com/advertisers/ad-exchange-networks

[xxxv] Global. "Global Radio". Thisisglobal.com. http://www.thisisglobal.com/radio/

[xxxvi] Shields, Ronan. "Programmatic, Coming to a Street Near You." ExchangeWire.com, July 2, 2015. https://www.exchangewire.com/blog/2015/07/02/programmatic-coming-to-a-street-near-you/

9 788026 096115